GLUTEN-FREE
& VEGAN
BREAD

GLUTEN-FREE & VEGAN BREAD

Artisanal Recipes to Make at Home

JENNIFER KATZINGER

Photographs by Kathryn Barnard

SASQUATCH BOOKS
SEATTLE

For Lillian

✦ ✦ ✦ ✦ ✦

Printed in China

Published by Sasquatch Books
17 16 15 14 13 12   9 8 7 6 5 4 3 2 1

Cover and interior photographs: Kathryn Barnard
Cover and interior design: Anna Goldstein

Library of Congress Cataloging-in-Publication Data is available.

ISBN-13: 978-1-57061-780-5
Sasquatch Books

1904 Third Avenue, Suite 710
Seattle, WA 98101
(206) 467-4300
www.sasquatchbooks.com
custserv@sasquatchbooks.com

CONTENTS

RECIPE LIST

FLATBREADS

BATTER BREADS

QUICK BREADS

ACKNOWLEDGMENTS

THERE ARE SO MANY PEOPLE to whom I feel gratitude, that have influenced the turn of events to this point such that I have found myself authoring a third cookbook! First and foremost, thank you, Joseph. Thank you for sharing your life with me, I love you. Thank you for courageously and lovingly inspiring me to go after what I find to be meaningful. Thank you, Lilli. Thank you for always showing me new ways. This most precious and sacred gift of being your mommy and getting to know you every day, I cherish with all my heart. I love you, Lilli. Thank you, Gabrielle Anderson. I am so grateful for your friendship. Your pureness of heart, ardor for vitality, and nurturing presence enkindle such joy in Joseph, Lilli, and me. Thank you to all of Lilli's grandparents, aunts, uncles, and cousins. All your love and support is deeply felt. Thank you to the entire Sasquatch Books team: working with all of you is such a creative, productive, and joyful experience. Thank you, Susan Roxborough, for your guidance and for having the confidence in me to author a third book. Thank you, Rachelle Longé, for your graceful and instructive communication. Thank you, Anna Goldstein, for your beautiful design work. It is such a great pleasure to work with you. Thank you, Kathryn Barnard. Your photos make my books come to life in such artful and mouthwatering ways. It is an honor to have your involvement. There are so many people I haven't mentioned whose enthusiasm, friendship, and support have fueled the manifestation of this book. I hope when you read this you all know who you are and how grateful I am.

INTRODUCTION

WRITING THIS GLUTEN-FREE, VEGAN bread-baking book has been an earnest goal of mine for some time. Making bread at home has the power to transport you right into the most precious of places. There you will find yourself at your kitchen counter, completely immersed in the act of working with your hands, creating a dough with all your senses engaged that will be baked into a nourishing choice staple for you and your family. Bread has a rare and special presence in our lives as a food we hold in the highest esteem, a food that has been in existence since ancient times and is still present at most meals, whether fancy or casual, across numerous cultures. Sharing bread with others is a very common and yet a very sacred experience.

It also seems that there is a growing movement afoot. More and more people are taking time to participate in the most simple yet fulfilling acts of living: baking their own bread, shopping at farmers' markets, getting involved with community gardens, making music, and more.

Being able to bake your own bread with ingredients full of life-giving sustenance is very empowering. And, it can be extremely gratifying to bake your own gluten-free and vegan bread. I am going to go so far as to say that right now it is even essential if you want your bread to be of high quality. I am acutely aware of the gluten-free breads available in the supermarkets and how they are very rarely also vegan or even dairy- and egg-free. They also tend to be laden with cornstarch and high fructose corn syrup, are heavy on guar and xanthan gums, lacking in whole grains (and therefore fiber), and aren't usually organic. I believe you will benefit on so many life-enriching levels by baking your own bread. If you are someone who has celiac disease; are gluten-free and vegan; or even just avoid eggs, dairy, or gluten due to allergies or food sensitivities (but you love healthy bread), I believe you will use these recipes often. Partaking in this age-old tradition of baking, you will be connecting with the timeless experience of transforming flour and water into bread to be shared.

Upon commencing the creation and collection of these bread recipes, I drew upon my first gluten-free and vegan bread experiences from back when I started the Flying Apron Bakery. That was a time when I predominantly used single-strain yeast, baking soda, and some batter bread techniques. Although I had always wanted to be intimately involved in creating and working with a gluten-free sourdough starter, this seemed like too much of an undertaking when I ran the bakery—in part, I suppose, because we had our hands full with the production of so many pastries. I am now thrilled to say I have a gorgeous gluten-free sourdough starter in my refrigerator, and it is such a joy to be independent (when I want to be) of store-bought yeast, and to be enjoying bread that has the tangy taste of a slight fermentation. I also relish knowing that my family is reaping the benefits from breads that have many strains of yeast instead of just one, as well as containing all those extra B vitamins.

The spectrum of recipes in this book covers lighter soft sandwich breads, old-world flatbreads, crusty baguettes, sweet yeasted breads, very hearty whole grain breads, breads made with their own wild starter, wholesome batter breads, and instantly gratifying quick breads. With every recipe my desire has been to create something beautiful, delicious, and nurturing. If you are a health nut like me, you will probably find the wild starter breads and batter breads to be the healthiest in the book; still, all of the breads here are beneficial and health-promoting, made with wholesome ingredients that are nutrient dense, have very little added sweetener, and use minimal xanthan gum, when it is called for at all.

The About the Ingredients section (page xix) dives into the rich details about each wonderful wholesome flour, root, seed, sweetener, and oil, affirming how exciting it is to be making and savoring this gluten-free, vegan bread. Even the lighter yeasted breads, which offer a little less fiber, are made with flours such as teff, amaranth, sorghum, and quinoa. All of these grains are valued for their unique content of minerals and vitamins, and are naturally high in protein and fiber. You will also notice chia seeds and flax meal in many ingredient lists: both are powerhouses for fiber and nutrition. Delving into and exploring each ingredient in order to compile this section of the book was extremely gratifying and enlightening.

On that note, I would like to draw your attention to three ingredients that appear in this book's recipes: tapioca flour, arrowroot, and xanthan gum. The first two I make special mention of because I have changed my tune slightly about these starches. If you are acquainted with my other two cookbooks you may recall my enthusiasm over recipes being free of starches and made only with whole grain flours. I still very much prefer whole grain flours to refined flours; however, I have included tapioca flour and arrowroot in a good number of the bread recipes here because I wanted to provide a range of breads that varied from being quite light to very hearty. I also took a closer look at these two ingredients and was delightfully surprised to learn that they have some beneficial qualities and are made in what appears to be very natural ways. Arrowroot, for example, is a perennial plant that is made into a powder by drying the juice extracted from its roots. It is high in vitamin B6, folate, thiamin, niacin, iron, phosphorus, potassium, and manganese. Tapioca flour is extracted from the cassava root, and while it certainly isn't packed with nutrition, it does contain a bit of folate and a fair amount of iron as well as other trace minerals.

As for xanthan gum, you will notice there are many recipes that contain a teaspoon of xanthan gum to yield one loaf of bread. You will also notice a fair number of recipes that call for no xanthan gum. This can be explained very simply: when I could achieve fantastic results without it, I didn't include it. This was most often the case with the flatbreads, batter breads, wild starter breads, and many of the quick breads. In other recipes I found it to be a necessary ingredient in order to yield loaves of bread that held together well and had a smooth crust. (Should you choose to omit the xanthan gum from any recipe, I think you will find the bread still most toothsome, but its appearance will be extremely crackly on the crust, and you may achieve slightly less oven spring.) In researching this ingredient, I have found varying opinions about its inclusion in our foods. It is certainly widely used, as it can be found in most prepared salad dressings, ice creams, gluten-free baked goods, and more. However there are instances of people voicing their discomfort after ingesting xanthan gum, describing symptoms such as severe bloating. Most commercial xanthan gum is a byproduct of bacteria that feed on corn, with some derived from the bacteria feeding on wheat. Intuitively, it does not feel like a food. However, in writing this book, I learned that it does occur in nature and can be found on cabbage leaves. Knowing this puts me somewhat at ease, because perhaps the problem is in having too heavy a dose of xanthan gum in our foods. I cannot speak as an authority on the matter, but I do feel a great sense of responsibility in bringing to light these various concerns, as xanthan gum is used in many of the recipes here. Please do consider this before proceeding and learn more by reading the introduction to the Wild Starter Breads chapter (page 69).

Now that you have an overview of what this book offers and an informed awareness as to why you will benefit from these recipes, I would like to conclude by sharing that I have taken great teachings and ideas from many other bread book authors, including those writing about gluten breads. I looked especially to Peter Reinhart and Andrew Whitley's respective books for wild starter and fermentation instructions, as well as for a more thorough and in-depth understanding of what happens on a molecular and biological level with yeast and bacteria as they feed on starches and proteins. Of course these books were referring to glutinous grains, but they helped me to understand and speculate on a much deeper level why my gluten-free doughs were reacting so differently, and why new methodologies are called for to create better gluten-free, vegan bread. (You may be surprised at my instructions regarding the dough rising period!) I imagine there has been a certain disrespect for gluten-free breads in the baking community because they are, for the most part, trying to imitate wheat breads (with the exception of flatbreads made from cassava, injera bread, arepas, oat farls, corn tortillas, and some purely oat breads), using a great many ingredients and additives to do so. In comparison to the almost four thousand years bakers and scientists have been working with wheat and studying the many gorgeous artisan ways one can utilize forms and flavors from wild starters, very little attention has been devoted to gluten-free breads. It feels like we are just at the beginning of a long journey through uncharted waters, navigating the use of gluten-free flours in a way that incorporates wild yeasts and whole grain flours without relying on eggs or dairy, or large amounts of guar and xanthan gums. With the recipes included here, I believe we have made terrific headway! I have taken inspiration from breads of different heritages, and have to some extent tried to replicate a texture, taste, and experience that transports us and offers a connection to tradition. My goal was to do so in a way that had great respect for each ingredient and to use the fewest ingredients possible, giving the breads more integrity for what they were while still drawing upon an ancient semblance. Because I am not a scientist, I am unable to provide as much of the chemistry involved with steps taken in each recipe, but I have some strong theories and discoveries to share, plus interesting evidence to back them up! Through much trial and error, I present you with the tastiest of these gluten-free and vegan bread recipes. Happy baking!

About the RECIPES

LIKE THE RECIPES in my other books, the ones you'll find here probably look different from those found in other vegan or gluten-free cookbooks. Some of the characteristics that make the recipes in this collection unique are detailed here.

✦ ✦ ✦ ✦ ✦

SOY-FREE, DAIRY-FREE, AND EGG-FREE

All of the recipes in this book are gluten-free, plant-based, and made from whole foods. So that they can be enjoyed by all, the recipes are also very allergy friendly: they are soy-free, dairy-free, and egg-free—a rare combination.

I've noticed over the years that many vegan cookbooks depend heavily on soy as a substitute for eggs and milk. While soy is a wonderfully nutritious food, there are many people who suffer from soy allergies, so its use is omitted here. Aside from being less allergenic, these soy-, dairy-, and egg-free foods have the added bonus of being cholesterol-free. I've received a lot of positive feedback from people who have really appreciated the absence of soy in my recipes.

✦ ✦ ✦ ✦ ✦

WHOLE GRAINS AND LOCAL, ORGANIC PRODUCTS

Many gluten-free recipes rely heavily on eggs, egg replacement products, and white rice flour. You will notice that most of the flours used in these recipes are made primarily with whole grains. Given the health benefits of whole grains, I strongly prefer their use over processed and refined flours and starches.

The sweeteners used in many cookbooks tend to be refined and unhealthy. Instead of those, the recipes that follow utilize natural sweeteners such as maple syrup, Sucanat, date sugar, and molasses.

Michael Pollan (author of *Food Rules* and *In Defense of Food*) emphasizes the importance of using as many local ingredients as possible, and I would like to do the same. Of course, "local" ingredients vary from one place to another; I advise you to select and support the local options that are available to you.

Finally, note that none of the recipes call specifically for organic ingredients. That said, I do enthusiastically encourage you to choose organic ingredients whenever possible. When you choose organic ingredients, you are selecting foodstuffs free from harmful pesticides as well as pulled from a richer soil, which in turn provides more minerals and nutrients for our bodies.

About the
INGREDIENTS

IF YOU HAVE CELIAC DISEASE OR ARE GLUTEN-INTOLERANT, it's a good idea to consistently check that the sources of your ingredients are safe from gluten contamination. There are some very trustworthy brands such as Bob's Red Mill and Lundberg, for example. Some companies that sell brown rice flour, bean flours, oats, or other would-be gluten-free ingredients mill where other glutenous grains are milled, making what should be a gluten-free ingredient a carrier of gluten. Thankfully, awareness of gluten intolerance has grown so tremendously that buying gluten-free ingredients has become increasingly easy over the years. Check with the Gluten Intolerance Group (www.gluten .net) for sources of gluten-free ingredients near you.

Some of the ingredients in this cookbook may require a trip to a specialty store or may need to be ordered online. Others are common enough to be shelved in the health food section of large grocery stores.

ACTIVE DRY YEAST is a living organism, a microorganism that transforms sugar into carbon dioxide, making the bubbles in dough that we rely on to produce light loaves of bread. It is a very fine, concentrated, and potent store-bought single strain of yeast that has been dried but still has live cells. (I find Fleischmann's RapidRise instant yeast to yield the most consistent results.)

ALMOND MEAL, which is made from ground sweet almonds, has a consistency much like cornmeal. It adds a rich nutty taste to breads and baked goods as well as moistness, and is loaded with vitamin E and magnesium.

AMARANTH FLOUR has a very distinct and delightfully earthy flavor and is high in fiber (with twice the fiber of wheat, for example) and protein. Amaranth is actually not a grass (like wild rice) or even a grain, but a broad-leafed plant that is related to Swiss chard and spinach! The top flowers of the shoots are abundant with the seeds that are ground into amaranth flour. Amaranth is rich in lysine, an amino acid lacking in most grains. It is also an excellent source of iron and calcium and is high in vitamin E.

ARROWROOT is a unique starch in that it contains calcium ash and trace sea minerals. It is a fine powder with a consistency that lends lightness to baked goods and breads. Arrowroot is surprisingly quite unrefined: The rootstalk of the arrowroot plant is simply dried and ground to make the powder.

BROWN RICE FLOUR has a very delicate flavor and is a terrific source of fiber. It also contains some protein and significant amounts of the minerals selenium and magnesium.

BUCKWHEAT has a very distinguishable and particularly hearty taste. It is actually an herbal plant; its seeds are milled to create a beautiful dark-colored flour. Buckwheat is very easily digested and is considered a complete protein in that it contains all eight essential amino acids. It is high in fiber as well as B vitamins and is also a wonderful source of calcium, phosphorous, and magnesium. Because it is digested slowly, you are more likely to feel very satisfied and full after eating something made with buckwheat.

CHIA SEEDS, from the desert of southern Mexico, are from a plant that belongs to the mint family. What is so remarkable about chia seeds is that when soaked in water, they transform into a very thick gelatin. They are a fantastic source of soluble fiber and work beautifully at slowing down the conversion of carbohydrates into sugar in the digestive tract. Chia seeds are also a amazing source of omega-3 fatty acids. I find them to be a very healthful ingredient that adds binding ability to gluten-free dough.

COCONUT FLOUR, high in fiber and protein, has a slightly sweet taste and adds body to baked goods. It is made from the fiber of coconut meat after its oil has been extracted.

CORNMEAL is dried corn kernels that have been ground into flour. I prefer the cornmeal that contains the bran and the germ as it is more nutritious. Bob's Red Mill (www.bobsredmill.com) has an excellent organic cornmeal that contains both the bran and the germ. Cornmeal is a very tasty and potent source of fiber. In addition, folate and the antioxidant beta-cryptoxanthin are found in significant amounts.

DATE SUGAR is an unprocessed sugar made from dehydrated dates that are ground into small bits. Date sugar is high in fiber and contains many vitamins and minerals, including iron.

EVAPORATED CANE JUICE comes from sugar cane, as does refined sugar; however, evaporated cane juice is processed to a much lesser degree so it retains more of the sugarcane's nutrients, such as riboflavin.

FLAX SEEDS and **FLAX MEAL** are super-rich in alpha linolenic acid, an omega-3 fatty acid, as well as lignans and fiber. They are terrific for adding a binding quality to egg-free baked goods and breads, along with a small but significant flavor and texture. They are a wonderfully healthful ingredient with potent anti-inflammatory properties and are associated with a reduced risk of cancer.

GARBANZO BEAN FLOUR is a great choice for creating substance in gluten-free doughs and adding moisture and a subtly sweet, beany flavor. It is high in protein, fiber, and iron. Something fascinating I just learned is that garbanzo beans also contain molybdenum, which helps the body rid itself of sulfites.

HAZELNUT FLOUR is a slightly sweet and nutty flour that adds great texture and exceptional flavor to baked goods. Hazelnuts and hazelnut flour are rich in vitamin E as well as potassium and magnesium.

MAPLE SYRUP comes from the sap that is extracted from maple trees and then boiled to create the topping we often drizzle on pancakes. Enjoying a little bit of maple syrup is a wonderful way to receive the trace minerals zinc and manganese.

MILLET FLOUR comes from the seeds of a cereal grass that is closely related to sorghum. It is a fine source of protein, potassium, iron, and magnesium and imparts a quality of lightness to baked goods and breads.

OATS that are grown and milled segregated from glutinous grains are considered gluten-free. Usually oats are milled in mills that also grind wheat, barley, rye, and the like, therefore picking up trace amounts of gluten. Thankfully, gluten-free oats are widely available now. Oats are rich in B vitamins, iron, calcium, vitamin E, and very high in fiber and protein! Since they are a high-fiber food that is digested slowly, they reduce cholesterol and regulate blood sugar.

POTATO FLOUR is made from ground dehydrated potatoes. It adds moisture and body to baked goods and is very high in potassium.

POTATO STARCH, made by extracting the starch from potatoes, is very mild in taste. It is high in vitamin B6, potassium, thiamin, magnesium, niacin, phosphorous, and manganese.

QUINOA FLOUR, made from ground quinoa seeds, is a unique flour with a mildly nutty and addictive taste. It is one of the most nutritious flours one could possibly use. It has more protein than any other flour and is high in zinc, iron, calcium, B vitamins, phosphorus, potassium, magnesium, and manganese.

SORGHUM FLOUR (also known as milo flour) comes from the whole grain kernel of sorghum. Nutritionally sorghum is much like corn but higher in protein and fat. It contains many minerals such as potassium, calcium, niacin, and phosphorous, has a very mellow taste, and adds body to gluten-free breads and baked goods.

SUCANAT is made from dehydrating juice from the sugar cane. It has a full-bodied flavor and is much less refined than other sugars.

TAPIOCA FLOUR is made from cassava root, which is boiled and dried and then powdered. Tapioca contains no protein, but it does provide a little bit of folate and a fair amount of iron, as well as other trace minerals such as calcium, magnesium, phosphorous, potassium, zinc, copper, manganese, and selenium. I find its addition to breads contributes a delicious, golden crust and often creates a lighter texture, as well as toning down the flavors of stronger flours.

TEFF FLOUR is a flour milled from the North African whole grain cereal known as teff, the world's smallest whole grain. Teff flour has a delightful, wholesome, yet subtle taste. The protein content of teff flour is exceptional in that it contains all eight essential amino acids. Teff flour is also rich in fiber, calcium, copper, and iron. It is also very high in lysine, an important amino acid frequently lacking in other grains.

WILD YEASTS consist of many strains of yeast and can be captured at home from the unique microorganisms floating around in your kitchen! To learn more, refer to page 71 for a comprehensive tutorial. Some wild yeasts have been passed down for hundreds of years and are valued for their flavor and connection to the past. These yeasts are full of B vitamins.

XANTHAN GUM is used to add elasticity to gluten-free doughs. It is a natural byproduct of *Xanthomonas campestris*, which feeds on fermenting plant matter—often corn, but sometimes wheat. Because of this, be sure to know your source of xanthan gum to avoid trace amounts of gluten. This process of fermentation is similar to the fermentation of beer, cheese, and yogurt.

YEASTED BREADS

I **HAVE A BREAD CONFESSION.** I have what some may think an outrageous method for making gluten-free yeasted breads that is unique and contrary to what works so beautifully for gluten breads. Many gluten-free bread bakers (including myself) start with the process, methodology, and intuition of traditional bread baking when that may not be necessary. But before I lay out this unique gluten-free bread process, let me shed some light on yeast and enzymes.

Yeast is an expeditiously reproducing fungus that is ubiquitous in our environment; when used in baking, it causes breads to rise in the most delicious of manners. This is due to the fascinating chemical reaction that begins with yeast reproduction. Yeast reproduction (while not very romantic but quite effective) is called *budding*. In budding, a yeast cell wall expands until it detaches itself from the main cell. This new cell then grows and follows the pattern of detaching—and the budding process continues.

Amidst all this growth and budding, the yeast cells are simultaneously producing enzymes, the very complex proteins that (very simply put) break larger molecules into smaller ones so that they are easily digested. One yeast enzyme called *invertase* breaks sucrose into glucose and fructose; then the yeast goes to town eating up the glucose now so readily available. Through this digestion and consumption, wonderful bubbles of carbon dioxide and very small amounts of ethanol (alcohol) are released. It is because of this rather gassy affair that our bread dough rises.

As of late, all the rage in the artisan wheat bread world is about slow fermentation, a process that allows the dough to have an extended period of time in a cool environment to rise and gain flavor. The enzymes take the stage as they tirelessly and diligently break down the starches; meanwhile the yeast cells are mostly dormant, sleeping in the chilly air. As the enzymes work, the starches are turned into various sugars that eventually metamorphose into a taste experience that is deliciously rich and elaborate. The baker however, must take the lead in this *couru* (dance) with the enzymes if there is going to be a favorable outcome. Since the enzymes would (rather rudely) dine on so much of the starch and protein if left unchecked, without the baker's intervention there wouldn't be the fine balance and ratio of starch to protein to sugar to yield a structure of dough (even in the case of a glutinous dough) to create a loaf of bread.

All this discussion of enzymes and yeast is indeed leading up to my gluten-free bread confession. Bear with me as I give just a few more details about gluten. My goal is that all this background information will provide a basic understanding of how traditional ingredients are transformed into breads so that we can begin to deduce why a new method is called for when working with gluten-free flours.

Gluten is a blend of the proteins gliadin and glutenin, which are attached to starch in the endosperm of many grass-related grains such as wheat, barley, spelt, and rye. When the grain's flour is combined with liquid, the gliadin and glutenin bond to make the durable and resilient protein we call gluten. It is because of this strong web of proteins that glutinous doughs have such exquisite elasticity. This elasticity provides both the room and the confinement to trap the gassy carbon dioxide air bubbles given off during fermentation. When a glutinous dough is baked, the result is a fine loaf full of air pockets, a well-kept shape, and a chewy texture.

So what happens when one wants to create a gluten-free bread that is also full of air pockets and has a beautiful shape and a toothsome texture? Here is my confession: After my yeasted bread doughs are shaped, they are not left on the counter to rise and ferment. Instead they are placed directly into the hot oven to bake. How scandalous this feels to bypass such a sacred tradition of rising and fermentation! Yet time after time these gluten-free recipes perform so much more pleasingly when this supposedly crucial step is omitted. Even the dough in the wild starter chapter's recipes (that are made from your very own starter) go directly into the oven rather than fermenting/rising again.

You may be wondering if these gluten-free vegan yeasted breads rise at all, and if so how this occurs. You may also be wondering why these gluten-free doughs perform in such a different manner than gluten doughs if left to ferment and rise. First of all, indubitably these yeasted bread doughs rise. Upon entering the hot oven, the dough's temperature—and therefore the yeast's temperature—rises. Bear in mind that yeast is very much influenced by temperature. In fact, intense heat causes the yeast cells to go into an accelerated state of feeding, devouring sugars and emitting carbon dioxide gases. This impressive increase in the dough's mass upon initial baking is called *oven spring*. Eventually, the yeasts cells perish when the temperature of the dough reaches 140 degrees F. At this time the bread dough stops rising and begins transforming into bread as the baking continues. Both glutinous breads and gluten-free breads benefit and rely (to different extents) on oven spring. One of the major differences with my gluten-free bread recipes is that I rely exclusively on oven spring for rise.

I have a theory as to why my gluten-free vegan bread recipes do so well without rising, as well as why the fermentation/rising period prior to baking doesn't yield the satisfactory results that it does for traditional gluten breads and other gluten-free bread recipes that contain eggs and large amounts of xanthan gum.

Let's compare gluten doughs to gluten-free doughs first. Gluten is a unique protein in that it builds and rebuilds bonds with other protein molecules such as gliadin and glutenin (to name just a few). In this reassembling process a very tenacious, intricate, complex, and tight structure is created that can withstand great enzyme activity. Remember, enzymes really go to work during the fermentation process of traditional breads, breaking apart peptide bonds between amino acids. This enzyme activity over time will greatly affect the bread dough's flavor, as well as its structural strength.

Because of this, the length of time a gluten dough ferments can be much longer than a gluten-free dough. Here is my theory as to why: Activity by *protease*, an enzyme that works on protein chains, is radically increased when acting on gluten-free ingredients. In comparison, protease activity in wheat dough is minimal (and is often relied upon by wheat bakers only to soften the dough while it rests prior to kneading). But because doughs that are gluten-free have so little structure to begin with, if they are allowed to ferment and rise on the counter, the enzyme activity will increase, and protease will regretfully leave something that is so crumbly and weak in structure that one could hardly call it a bread at all. Hence my method for popping gluten-free bread dough directly into the oven and relying on oven spring from the yeast for risen bread.

Let us now address the vast majority of gluten-free bread recipes that call for a rising period: they contain eggs and in most cases three times the amount of xanthan gum my recipes do. Both ingredients contribute greatly to the dough's ability to trap gases and provide structure and elasticity. The eggs offer strong binding properties and are used as a form of leavening. The xanthan gum serves as a replacement for gluten, providing viscosity and with that, the pliability to trap yeasty gases. I view xanthan gum as an additive rather than a food (it's likely that most people do as well, but disregard this in order to achieve more desirable results) and I feel it should be used only in small amounts. Given that, I am uncomfortable using a tablespoon of xanthan gum in each bread loaf, and of course want to avoid eggs since these are vegan breads—so I prefer other ways of leavening.

Which brings us full circle in this new method of relying on oven spring for leavening and using the hot oven to bake structure into the bread. To reiterate: Rather than letting the dough rise, or depending on extra xanthan gum and eggs to withstand the enzyme activity taking place in gluten-free dough, I rely

on the accelerated yeast activity. This occurs when the dough initially enters the hot oven, and as it bakes into a bread that holds together so exquisitely.

Finally, these recipes are a whole lot of fun! They are made with very little effort and offer great fulfillment on many levels. You will find savory and sweet yeasted breads, both drawing from older bread-making traditions across many cultures. Naturally, they are not exact replicas of traditional wheat breads, given that their main ingredients are so anatomically different. Be that as it may, rest assured that the recipes that follow will manifest into the most delicious of gluten-free and vegan breads, made by your very own hands!

✦ ✦ ✦ ✦ ✦

YEASTED BREAD TIPS AND TECHNIQUES

Now that you are familiar with relying on oven spring for rise (bypassing a leavening period in a warm environment), let me share a few helpful tips for handling yeast doughs and working with the ingredients.

In almost all of the recipes, chia seeds are called for. Please be sure to soak the seeds for at least 15 minutes. In fact, because these recipes come together in less time than you may expect, go ahead and let the chia seeds and water have a 10-minute head start prior to starting the other steps. The viscous, thick slurry that develops in this time really makes the doughs sturdier and allows for more gases to be trapped during oven spring.

Let's discuss preheating the oven. Many of the recipes call for a water bath, which does wonders for the bread! The steam creates a gorgeous crust that you will be so proud of. It is best to place the water bath in the oven before preheating it, because you want to quickly pop the bread into the hot oven so as to prevent too much hot air from escaping. If you are juggling both the water bath and bread, the oven temperature is bound to decrease. Also, it's best to have a steamy environment in the oven as soon as the bread enters. I like to use a ceramic or glass pie plate to hold water for my water bath.

A quick tip about measuring flour, which I imagine will be helpful for novice bakers. For the greatest accuracy when measuring, spoon the flour into the cup with a big scoop. Go ahead and overfill the measuring cup. Next, level off the flour with a swipe of the straight side of a butter knife blade, ensuring consistent measurement.

I also find it helpful to use three bowls (when chia seeds are called for) in order to keep the measured ingredients temporarily separated into three groups. One small bowl for the chia seeds and water; a large bowl for the flours, flax meal, salt, and xanthan gum; and another large bowl for the water, oil, sweetener and yeast. If you have an upright mixer, go ahead and use the mixer's bowl for the water, oil, sweetener, and yeast.

After all of the dry ingredients are measured, do take some time to combine them with a mixing spoon, so that they all mix evenly into the dough (this is most important for the recipes that call for xanthan gum). After combining the dry ingredients, measure the water into the large bowl. Room temperature filtered water is preferable, but tap water will work. Because we are relying on oven spring (that is really when we want the yeast to be the most active) it is better to err on the side of cooler water than warmer water. Add to this water the active dry yeast, oil, and sweetener and stir gently to combine. Then go ahead and add your wonderful, thick, gelatinous goo of soaking chia seeds, followed by your dry ingredients. If using an upright mixer (a regular paddle works fine), combine the dough on slow speed, pulsing the mixer by turning it off and on, just until the dough forms. This won't take very long; just a minute or two will do.

As for handling the dough, minimal handling is optimal. Really what you want to do is shape the dough and not actually knead it. Usually this is done on a work surface dusted with flour; brown rice flour is a terrific option for shaping because it is light in color and less expensive than some of the other more unique flours called for. (I've made recommendations for each recipe as appropriate.) For a boule shape, simply turn the dough onto a lightly floured surface, and spin the ball around a few times, tucking the edges under, to achieve a smooth, round shape (as if it had been sitting in a bowl). For a batard shape, similarly turn the dough onto your floured surface and lightly roll it just until you have an oblong oval shape with tapered ends. Then transfer the dough to a prepared sheet pan (that is, a pan lined with parchment paper, lightly oiled, or generously dusted with flour to prevent the dough from sticking). For batons and baguettes, I like to shape the dough right on the sheet pan. For this, you'll need a generous amount of brown rice flour on the pan so the dough doesn't stick. With very little handling, roll the dough back and forth until you have a "snake" that runs the length of a sheet pan, about 18 inches by 13 inches, called a half-sheet pan.

What comes next is one of my favorite parts of the process: scoring the dough. Scoring prevents the bread from tearing as it rises and bakes, providing an artfully defined space for extra gas to escape. To score a gluten-free dough, sink your knife in a touch more than you would for a wheat dough. Just under ¼ inch will be just right. Sometimes I like to browse pictures of baked bread to admire the many different scoring designs. A simple semicircle on a boule is beautiful, and so are three curved lines stemming from one point, suggesting something like a tree branch. Crisscross lines creating diamonds is another classic example. On my batards, I like to score one simple straight line down the side of the loaf. For baguettes and batons, several just slightly angled scores running down the loaf on the diagonal is very traditional and lovely.

I've been very careful in creating these recipes to provide the exact baking times to yield loaves of bread baked to perfection. That said, every oven is different, and depending on the weather, ingredients can measure differently or be affected by moisture in the air, or lack thereof. Because of this, baking times may vary ever so slightly. So I recommend using an instant-read thermometer, which will read the internal temperature of your bread. When the temperature is in the range of 205 to 210 degrees F, you will know with certainty that your bread is done. I like to pick a discreet spot to insert the thermometer, usually on the underside of the loaf.

One final note: Please be aware that these doughs will be a little bit more wet and loose than standard wheat bread doughs, but are still sturdy enough to handle and shape.

You are now ready to begin. I am so excited for you to enjoy these recipes!

✦ Country Batard ✦

Ah, the ever so light and tasty batard. A touch of almond meal makes such a tooth-some contribution to this casual yet exquisite loaf. I am so struck by tapioca flour's ability to create caramelized golden crusts that taste wonderful; this batard really shows off that quality with its abundance of crust.

◇◇◇◇◇◇◇◇◇◇◇◇◇◇◇◇◇◇◇◇◇ **MAKES 1 MEDIUM LOAF** ◇◇◇◇◇◇◇◇◇◇◇◇◇◇◇◇◇◇◇◇◇

2 tablespoons chia seeds

½ cup water

1 cup brown rice flour

1 cup tapioca flour

½ cup garbanzo bean flour

½ cup millet flour

½ cup almond meal

1 teaspoon sea salt

1 teaspoon xanthan gum

1 envelope (2¾ teaspoons) active dry yeast

1 cup room temperature filtered water

3 tablespoons extra-virgin olive oil

2 tablespoons maple syrup

Poppy or sesame seeds, for sprinkling (optional)

1. Soak the chia seeds in the ½ cup water for at least 15 minutes. Preheat the oven to 450 degrees F and place a water bath on the bottom rack or the oven floor.

2. In a large mixing bowl, combine the brown rice flour, tapioca flour, garbanzo bean flour, millet flour, almond meal, salt, and xanthan gum.

3. In a separate large mixing bowl (or the bowl of a stand mixer), dissolve the yeast in the room temperature water. Add the olive oil and maple syrup. Just as the yeast begins to foam and feed on the maple syrup, about 3 minutes, add the combined dry ingredients and the chia seeds with their soaking liquid. Mix until a soft dough forms. You can do this by hand with a strong arm and a sturdy spoon, or with your stand mixer and the paddle attachment pulsed on low speed.

4. On a work surface generously dusted with brown rice flour, turn out the dough and gently form into a batard shape. Score by cutting 3 or 4 lines on the diagonal, or with 1 line that runs the length of the batard, just off center. Sprinkle with poppy or sesame seeds. Bake for 15 minutes. Decrease the temperature to 425 degrees F and bake for an additional 1 hour and 30 minutes, until golden brown and crusty.

⋆ Kalamata Olive Bread ⋆

This tasty and distinctive bread is light and chewy and the perfect backdrop for kal-amata olives, which many consider to be the most delicious olive of all. The dough comes together with ease, and is quite gratifying to make. When I first made the bread, I had in mind serving it for a family dinner. To my surprise and astonishment, the loaf was halfway devoured by my husband before we even sat down!

MAKES 1 MEDIUM LOAF

1 cup brown rice flour

1 cup tapioca flour

½ cup garbanzo bean flour

½ cup millet flour

½ cup almond meal

⅓ cup flax meal

1 teaspoon sea salt

1 teaspoon xanthan gum

½ cup kalamata olives, whole

1 envelope (2¾ teaspoons) active dry yeast

1½ cups room temperature filtered water

3 tablespoons canola oil

2 tablespoons Sucanat

1. Preheat the oven to 450 degrees F and place a water bath on the bottom rack or the oven floor. Lightly grease a sheet pan or line with parchment paper.

2. In a large mixing bowl, combine the brown rice flour, tapioca flour, garbanzo bean flour, millet flour, almond meal, flax meal, salt, and xanthan gum. Add the olives and gently mix.

3. In a separate large mixing bowl (or the bowl of a stand mixer), dissolve the yeast in the room temperature water. Add the canola oil and Sucanat. Just as the yeast begins to foam and feed on the Sucanat, about 3 minutes, add the combined dry ingredients with the olives. Mix thoroughly but just until the dough holds together. This will take just a few moments. You can do this by hand with a strong arm and a sturdy spoon, or with your stand mixer and the paddle attachment pulsed on low speed.

4. On a work surface generously dusted with brown rice flour, turn out the dough and gently form into a batard shape. Place on the prepared pan and score with one line that runs the length of the batard, just off center. Bake for 15 minutes. Decrease the temperature to 425 degrees F and bake for 1 hour. Decrease the temperature to 350 degrees F and bake for another 45 minutes, until golden brown and crusty. (Total baking time will be 2 hours.)

✦ Fougasse ✦

Every time I go to the farmers' market, I seek out the artisan bread stands just so I can cast my gaze upon the unique and beautiful fougasse. This gorgeous rustic Provençal bread is wonderfully chewy and flavorful, with an attractive shape meant to resemble a leaf or a ladder. I have yet to find a gluten-free fougasse at a bakery or farmers' market, but now I can make my own! This is a bread I am sure you will savor and take great pride in sharing with others. The recipe has room for variation: You may want to play around with adding rosemary or fresh thyme. Kalamata or green olives are also delectable.

◇◇◇◇◇◇◇◇◇◇◇◇◇◇◇◇◇◇◇◇◇◇◇ **MAKES 1 LARGE FOUGASSE** ◇◇◇◇◇◇◇◇◇◇◇◇◇◇◇◇◇◇◇◇◇◇◇

2 tablespoons chia seeds

½ cup water

1 cup teff flour

1 cup sorghum flour

1 cup tapioca flour

½ cup arrowroot

¼ cup flax meal

1 teaspoon sea salt

1 teaspoon xanthan gum

1 envelope (2¾ teaspoons) active dry yeast

1½ cups room temperature filtered water

3 tablespoons olive oil

2 tablespoons maple syrup

Coarse sea salt, for sprinkling

1. Soak the chia seeds in the ½ cup water for at least 15 minutes. Preheat the oven to 450 degrees F and place a water bath on the bottom rack or the oven floor. Line a sheet pan with parchment paper and dust generously with brown rice flour.

2. In a large mixing bowl, combine the teff flour, sorghum flour, tapioca flour, arrowroot, flax meal, salt, and xanthan gum.

3. In a separate large mixing bowl (or the bowl of a stand mixer), dissolve the yeast in the room temperature water. Add the olive oil and maple syrup. Just as the yeast begins to foam and feed on the maple syrup, about 3 minutes, add the combined dry ingredients and the chia seeds with their soaking liquid.

Mix together until you have achieved a soft dough. This will not take long. A stand mixer with a paddle attachment works well, but so will an old-fashioned wooden spoon and a tireless arm.

4. On a work surface generously dusted with brown rice flour, turn out the dough and gently shape into an oval. Transfer to the prepared sheet pan. Continue to flatten the dough to about 1 inch thick while maintaining an oval, leaf-like shape. You may need to wash, dry, and flour your hands a few times during this process.

5. Now for your artistic expression! There are a number of ways to shape and design fougasse. One way is like a ladder: With a floured sharp knife, cut four or five slices through the dough, starting about 1½ inches in from one end of the oval and ending about 1½ inches in from the other. Next, with floured clean hands, use your fingers to further separate these ladder sections, creating space between each "step."

6. I find the leaf-shaped fougasse to be very striking. There are two possibilities: Position the oval so that one of the short ends is nearest you. Make 3 or 4 diagonal, 1½-inch-long cuts on each side of an imaginary midline running the length of the oval. With floured clean hands, use your fingers to further separate these sections, creating space between each pocket to accentuate the look of a leaf.

7. The other way to form a leaf is to make a cut right down the midline of the oval before making your diagonal cuts, which should start 1 to 1½ inches away from the center cut. Then, as above, with floured clean hands, use your fingers to further separate the sections, creating space between each pocket to accentuate the look of a leaf.

8. Once the fougasse is shaped, sprinkle with coarse sea salt and place in the hot oven. Immediately reduce the temperature to 425 degrees F and bake for 1 hour and 10 minutes, until golden brown and crusty.

✦ Caraway Potato Bread ✦

A soft and hearty potato bread is such a warming treat, but is even better when bursting with tasty splashes of caraway. This recipe yields two charming loaves. To prepare a bit an advance, boil the potato for about 15 minutes and allow another 15 minutes for it to cool after mashing before making the dough.

◇◇◇◇◇◇◇◇◇◇◇◇◇◇◇◇◇◇◇◇ **MAKES 2 SMALL ROUND LOAVES** ◇◇◇◇◇◇◇◇◇◇◇◇◇◇◇◇◇◇◇◇

1½ cups teff flour

1 cup brown rice flour

1 cup tapioca flour

½ cup arrowroot

¼ cup flax meal

1½ teaspoons caraway seeds

1½ teaspoons sea salt

1 teaspoon xanthan gum

1 envelope (2¾ teaspoons) active dry yeast

1⅔ cups room temperature filtered water

3 tablespoons canola oil

2 tablespoons maple syrup

1 medium Yukon Gold potato (about 5 ounces), unpeeled, cooked, mashed, and cooled

1. Preheat the oven to 400 degrees F. Lightly grease a sheet pan or line with parchment paper.

2. In a large mixing bowl, combine the teff flour, brown rice flour, tapioca flour, arrowroot, flax meal, caraway seeds, salt, and xanthan gum.

3. In a separate large mixing bowl (or the bowl of a stand mixer), dissolve the yeast in the room temperature water. Add the canola oil and maple syrup. Just as the yeast begins to foam and feed on the maple syrup, about 3 minutes, add the combined dry ingredients and the cooled mashed potato. Mix just until a soft dough forms. You can do this by hand with a strong arm and a sturdy spoon, or with your stand mixer and the paddle attachment pulsed on low speed.

4. On a work surface generously dusted with brown rice flour or teff flour, turn out the dough and divide into 2 portions. Gently form each piece into a round

boule shape. Place the shaped dough on the prepared baking sheet and score each with 5 parallel lines running across the dough. Bake for 1 hour and 20 minutes, until golden brown and crusty.

✦ Straun Bread ✦

Straun bread is a hearty Scottish bread that traditionally includes a variety of freshly harvested whole grains. In this gluten-free version, I add wild rice to the dough, along with the tasty addition of walnuts. The walnuts are like a taste bud ovation to the sweet nuttiness of the wild rice. The small amount of amaranth flour is so very appropriate and delicious in this bread: Its flavorful presence is very much in synchronicity with the wholesome, earthy harvest theme. Please note that this bread bakes for an exceptionally long time, 4 hours. A mouthwatering, drawn-out time to be in anticipation of such an aromatic and gratifying loaf!

◇◇◇◇◇◇◇◇◇◇◇◇◇◇◇◇◇◇◇◇ **MAKES 1 LARGE LOAF** ◇◇◇◇◇◇◇◇◇◇◇◇◇◇◇◇◇◇◇◇

2 tablespoons chia seeds

½ cup water

1 cup teff flour, plus additional scant ½ cup for shaping the bread

1 cup tapioca flour

½ cup cooked wild rice, cooled

½ cup walnuts, chopped

¼ cup amaranth flour

¼ cup almond meal

¼ cup flax meal

1 teaspoon sea salt

½ teaspoon xanthan gum

1½ teaspoons active dry yeast

¾ cup room temperature filtered water

2 tablespoons canola oil

2 tablespoons maple syrup

1. Soak the chia seeds in the ½ cup water for at least 15 minutes. Preheat the oven to 425 degrees F. Lightly grease a sheet pan or line with parchment paper.

2. In a large mixing bowl, combine the teff flour, tapioca flour, wild rice, walnuts, amaranth flour, almond meal, flax meal, salt, and xanthan gum.

3. In a separate large mixing bowl (or the bowl of a stand mixer), dissolve the yeast in the room temperature water. Add the canola oil and maple syrup. Just as the yeast begins to foam and feed on the maple syrup, about 3 minutes, add the combined dry ingredients and the chia seeds with their soaking liquid. Mix well, just until the dough is soft and holding together. This will happen sooner

than you may expect. If you are using a stand mixer, insert the paddle attachment and pulse on low speed. Otherwise a wooden spoon will certainly do the trick.

4. On a work surface generously dusted with the additional teff flour, turn out the dough and gently form into a batard shape. Score with one line running the length of the batard, just off center. Place the shaped dough on the prepared sheet pan and pop into the hot oven. Once the oven door is closed, decrease the temperature to 350 degrees F and bake for 4 hours, until rich dark brown and firm to the touch.

✦ Russian Black Bread ✦

This full-bodied, ever so deeply flavorful bread is one of my favorites. The classic blend of Russian spices is exquisite, and the earthiness of the buckwheat flour and wild rice flour conjure up a similar taste experience to that of rye. While robust in flavor, the texture maintains a delightful lightness. Enjoy wholeheartedly! Appetit prikhodit vo vremya yedy!

‹‹‹‹‹‹‹‹‹‹‹‹‹‹‹‹‹‹‹‹‹‹ **MAKES 1 MEDIUM LOAF** ‹‹‹‹‹‹‹‹‹‹‹‹‹‹‹‹‹‹‹‹‹‹

¼ cup chia seeds

¾ cup water

1 cup sorghum flour

1 cup tapioca flour

½ cup arrowroot

¼ cup unsweetened cocoa powder

¼ cup wild rice flour

¼ cup buckwheat flour

2 teaspoons finely ground coffee

1 teaspoon caraway seeds

½ teaspoon fennel seeds

1 teaspoon sea salt

1 teaspoon xanthan gum

1 envelope (2¾ teaspoons) active dry yeast

¾ cup room temperature filtered water

¼ cup maple syrup

3 tablespoons extra-virgin olive oil

1 tablespoon molasses

1. Soak the chia seeds in the ¾ cup water for at least 15 minutes. Preheat the oven to 350 degrees F. Lightly grease a sheet pan and dust with buckwheat flour, or line with parchment paper.

2. In a large mixing bowl, combine the sorghum flour, tapioca flour, arrowroot, cocoa powder, wild rice flour, buckwheat flour, ground coffee, caraway seeds, fennel seeds, salt, and xanthan gum.

3. In a separate large mixing bowl (or the bowl of a stand mixer), dissolve the yeast in the room temperature water. Add the maple syrup, olive oil, and molasses. Just as the yeast begins to foam and feed on the maple syrup and molasses, about 3 minutes, add the combined dry ingredients and the chia

seeds with their soaking liquid. Combine well to the point where you have a lovely, pliable bread dough. Because my bread doughs are wetter than traditional bread doughs, you may be surprised at how quickly the dough comes together. Mix thoroughly until the dough holds together, at which point please do not continue mixing the dough. If you are using a stand mixer, insert the paddle attachment and pulse on low speed. Or if you prefer to use your arm and a wooden spoon, by all means enjoy this slightly slower but very effective way of mixing your bread dough!

4. With clean dry hands, shape the dough directly on your counter into a round. It is unlikely you will need any extra flour to do so. However, if you find that the dough is sticking a little bit, use just a touch of buckwheat flour to form. Once the bread is shaped, place it on the prepared sheet pan and score with four lines that form a square, centered directly on top. Bake for 2 hours and 20 minutes, until the exterior is firm to the touch.

✦ Broa ✦

Broa—Portuguese country bread—is outstanding for its lightness and abundance of cornmeal. Being a great fan of cornmeal's delicate flavor, I like that this yeasted bread highlights the golden grain with such balance and adroitness. In Portugal, broa is often served alongside soup. I fancy it toasted lightly for a simple breakfast.

<><><><><><><><><><><><><><><><><> **MAKES 1 MEDIUM LOAF** <><><><><><><><><><><><><><><><><>

1 cup brown rice flour

1 cup tapioca flour

1 cup medium grind cornmeal

½ cup garbanzo bean flour

1 teaspoon sea salt

1 teaspoon xanthan gum

1 envelope (2¾ teaspoons) active dry yeast

1¼ cups room temperature filtered water

3 tablespoons canola oil

2 tablespoons Sucanat

1. Preheat the oven to 350 degrees F. Lightly grease a sheet pan or line with parchment paper.

2. In a large mixing bowl, combine the brown rice flour, tapioca flour, cornmeal, garbanzo bean flour, salt, and xanthan gum.

3. In a separate large mixing bowl (or the bowl of a stand mixer), dissolve the yeast in the room temperature water. Add the canola oil and Sucanat. Just as the yeast begins to foam and feed on the Sucanat, about 3 minutes, add the combined dry ingredients. Mix until a soft dough forms. You can do this by hand with a strong arm and a sturdy spoon, or with your stand mixer and the paddle attachment pulsed on low speed.

4. On a work surface generously dusted with cornmeal, turn out the dough and gently form into a batard or round shape. Place on the prepared baking sheet. Score by cutting 3 or 4 lines on the diagonal, or with one line that runs the length of the batard, just off center. Score the round shape with a crisscross, forming a pattern of diamonds. Bake for 2 hours, until golden brown and crusty.

✦ Round White Bread ✦

This is an honorable, soft, light bread to be enjoyed by those who prefer white bread but appreciate the sustenance of whole grain flours such as teff, quinoa, and millet. With its semicircle score, this loaf rises in such a beautiful fashion, making an adorable puffed-up hat. I recommend shaping the dough using quinoa flour or brown rice flour for an attractive look.

◇◇◇◇◇◇◇◇◇◇◇◇◇◇◇◇◇◇◇ **MAKES 1 MEDIUM LOAF** ◇◇◇◇◇◇◇◇◇◇◇◇◇◇◇◇◇◇◇

2 tablespoons chia seeds

½ cup water

1 cup teff flour

1 cup tapioca flour

½ cup quinoa flour

½ cup millet flour

½ cup arrowroot

¼ cup flax meal

1 teaspoon sea salt

1 teaspoon xanthan gum

1 envelope (2¾ teaspoons) active dry yeast

1½ cups room temperature filtered water

3 tablespoons olive oil

2 tablespoons maple syrup

1. Soak the chia seeds in the ½ cup water for at least 15 minutes. Preheat the oven to 350 degrees F. Lightly grease a sheet pan or line with parchment paper.

2. In a large mixing bowl, combine the teff flour, tapioca flour, quinoa flour, millet flour, arrowroot, flax meal, salt, and xanthan gum.

3. In a separate large mixing bowl (or the bowl of a stand mixer), dissolve the yeast in the room temperature water. Add the olive oil and maple syrup. Just as the yeast begins to foam and feed on the maple syrup, about 3 minutes, add the combined dry ingredients and the chia seeds with their soaking liquid. Mix thoroughly but just until the dough holds together. This will take just a few moments. You can do this by hand with a strong arm and a sturdy spoon, or with your stand mixer and the paddle attachment pulsed on low speed.

4. On a work surface generously dusted with quinoa flour or brown rice flour, turn out the dough and gently form into a round boule shape. Place the shaped dough on the prepared sheet pan and score with a semicircle. Bake for 2 hours and 40 minutes, until golden brown and crusty.

✦ Petite Buckwheat Round ✦

This little gem of a bread has such diverse uses. It is perfect as part of a hot soup and salad dinner, toasted for breakfast, or made into a midday sandwich. Any way you slice it, you will be pleased with this soft and slightly nutty tasting loaf. I first made this bread for my dear friend Gabrielle who was visiting for afternoon tea. Warm out of the oven, we enjoyed it heartily, dipping it generously in extra-virgin olive oil.

◇◇◇◇◇◇◇◇◇◇◇◇◇◇◇◇◇◇◇◇ **MAKES 1 MEDIUM LOAF** ◇◇◇◇◇◇◇◇◇◇◇◇◇◇◇◇◇◇◇◇

2 tablespoons chia seeds

½ cup water

1 cup buckwheat flour

½ cup tapioca flour

¼ cup arrowroot

2 tablespoons flax meal

1 teaspoon salt

½ teaspoon xanthan gum

1½ teaspoons active dry yeast

½ cup room temperature
  filtered water

1 tablespoon maple syrup

1 tablespoon olive oil

1. Soak the chia seeds in the ½ cup water for at least 15 minutes. Preheat the oven to 425 degrees F. Lightly grease a sheet pan or line with parchment paper.

2. In a large mixing bowl, combine the buckwheat flour, tapioca flour, arrowroot, flax meal, salt, and xanthan gum.

3. In a separate large mixing bowl (or the bowl of a stand mixer), dissolve the yeast in the room temperature water. Add the maple syrup and olive oil. Just as the yeast begins to foam and feed on the maple syrup, about 3 minutes, add the combined dry ingredients and the chia seeds with their soaking liquid. Mix together until you have achieved a soft dough. This will not take long. You can do this by hand with a strong arm and a sturdy spoon, or with your stand mixer and the paddle attachment pulsed on low speed.

4. On a work surface generously dusted with brown rice flour, turn out the dough and gently form into a round boule shape. Place on the prepared sheet pan and score by cutting 3 curves stemming from one point, just like a beautiful tree branch might look. Place in the hot oven. Once the oven door is closed, decrease the temperature to 350 degrees F and bake for 2 hours, until dark brown and crusty.

✦ Pain de Campagne ✦

This lovely, full-bodied bread is very pleasing in that it is light yet quite abundant in many whole grain flours. Cornmeal within the dough and on the crust makes for a texture that is one of my personal favorites. Pain de campagne (country bread) is traditionally made with a young starter, or poolish, and baked in a very hot oven. My pain de campagne is made with dry yeast—but because of its boule shape, the many whole grain flours, and the light weight of the bread, I thought country bread was a fitting title.

◇◇◇◇◇◇◇◇◇◇◇◇◇◇◇◇◇◇ **MAKES 2 MEDIUM LOAVES** ◇◇◇◇◇◇◇◇◇◇◇◇◇◇◇◇◇◇

2 tablespoons chia seeds

½ cup water

1 cup arrowroot

¾ cup millet flour

¾ cup teff flour

½ cup almond meal

½ cup potato starch

⅓ cup flax meal

¼ cup amaranth flour

¼ cup quinoa flour

¼ cup cornmeal, plus ½ cup additional for shaping loaves

1 teaspoon sea salt, plus additional for sprinkling

1 teaspoon xanthan gum

1 envelope (2¾ teaspoons) active dry yeast

1½ cups room temperature filtered water

3 tablespoons olive oil

2 tablespoons maple syrup

1. Soak the chia seeds in the ½ cup water for at least 15 minutes. Preheat the oven to 425 degrees F. Lightly grease a sheet pan or line with parchment paper.

2. In a large mixing bowl combine the arrowroot, millet flour, teff flour, almond meal, potato starch, flax meal, amaranth flour, quinoa flour, ¼ cup cornmeal, salt, and xanthan gum.

3. In a separate large mixing bowl (or the bowl of a stand mixer), dissolve the yeast in the room temperature water. Add the olive oil and maple syrup. Just as the yeast begins to foam and feed on the maple syrup, about 3 minutes, add

the combined dry ingredients and the chia seeds with their soaking liquid. Mix just until a soft dough forms. You can do this by hand with a strong arm and a sturdy spoon, or with your stand mixer and the paddle attachment pulsed on low speed.

4. With the ½ cup cornmeal dusting your work surface, turn out the dough and divide into 2 equal portions. Shape each portion of dough into a round, using ample cornmeal to aid in the forming; this gives the exterior of the bread a delicious coarse texture. Place the unbaked rounds on the prepared pan and score each with a semicircle shape. Sprinkle with a little extra sea salt before popping into the hot oven. Once the oven door is closed, turn the temperature down to 350 degrees F and bake for 2 hours and 10 minutes, until golden brown and crusty.

✦ Multiple Grain Baguette ✦

There are a few baguette recipes in this book, varying from light to quite hearty. While this baguette contains multiple whole grains (with teff flour, legume flour, millet flour, and seeds), it is still a very light loaf due to the tapioca flour and potato flour. The shape of the baguette allows it to offer more crust than any other. I believe that may be why I am partial to the baguette—I just can't get enough crust!

〰〰〰〰〰〰〰〰〰〰〰〰〰〰 **MAKES 2 BAGUETTES** 〰〰〰〰〰〰〰〰〰〰〰〰〰〰

2 tablespoons chia seeds

½ cup water

1 cup teff flour

1 cup tapioca flour

½ cup potato flour

½ cup garbanzo bean flour

½ cup millet flour

¼ cup flax meal

1 teaspoon sea salt

1 teaspoon xanthan gum

1 envelope (2¾ teaspoons) active dry yeast

1½ cups room temperature filtered water

3 tablespoons canola oil

2 tablespoons maple syrup

Coarse sea salt, for sprinkling

Poppy seeds, for sprinkling

1. Soak the chia seeds in the ½ cup water for at least 15 minutes. Preheat the oven to 450 degrees F and place a water bath on the bottom rack or the oven floor. Line a sheet pan with parchment paper.

2. In a large mixing bowl, combine the teff flour, tapioca flour, potato flour, garbanzo bean flour, millet flour, flax meal, salt, and xanthan gum.

3. In a separate large mixing bowl (or the bowl of a stand mixer), dissolve the yeast in the room temperature water. Add the canola oil and maple syrup. Just as the yeast comes alive and begins to feed on the maple syrup, add the combined dry ingredients and the chia seeds with their soaking liquid. Mix well, just until the dough is soft and holding together. This will happen sooner than you may expect. You can do this by hand with a strong arm and a sturdy spoon, or with your stand mixer and the paddle attachment pulsed on low speed.

4. On a work surface generously dusted with brown rice flour or teff flour, turn out the dough and divide into 2 equal parts. Gently form each piece into a baton shape about the length of your sheet pan. I suggest beginning to roll out the baton on the counter and then transferring it to the prepared sheet where you can finish elongating the dough. Score the batons with parallel ¼-inch-deep lines across the dough on the diagonal, about 3 inches apart. Sprinkle with coarse sea salt and poppy seeds. Bake for 15 minutes. Decrease the temperature of the oven to 425 degrees F and bake for 1 hour and 15 minutes longer, until golden brown and crusty. Voila! Two crusty baguettes await you!

✦ Whole Grain Batons ✦

This is a softer baton, as it bakes at a slightly lower temperature than other baguette or baton recipes, which are traditionally baked between 400 and 500 degrees F. It is scrumptious in its own right and a bit different from the crusty batons that bake in a hotter oven. Every once in a while I replace 1 tablespoon of the maple syrup with 1 tablespoon molasses for a bread that's like a dark German vollkornbrot loaf! Either way, this is a terrific bread that can be enjoyed in many ways. Note: This recipe calls for finely ground chia seeds rather than whole ones as elsewhere in this book.

◇◇◇◇◇◇◇◇◇◇◇◇◇◇◇◇◇◇◇◇◇◇◇◇ **MAKES 2 LOAVES** ◇◇◇◇◇◇◇◇◇◇◇◇◇◇◇◇◇◇◇◇◇◇◇◇

2 tablespoons chia seeds, finely ground (can be store-bought finely ground)

½ cup water

2 cups brown rice flour

1 cup teff flour

½ cup millet flour

¼ cup flax meal

1 teaspoon sea salt

1 teaspoon xanthan gum

1 envelope (2¾ teaspoons) active dry yeast

1½ cups room temperature filtered water

3 tablespoons extra-virgin olive oil

2 tablespoons maple syrup

Coarse sea salt, for sprinkling

1. Soak the chia seeds in the ½ cup water for at least 15 minutes. Preheat the oven to 350 degrees F. Line a sheet pan with parchment paper.

2. In a large mixing bowl, combine the brown rice flour, teff flour, millet flour, flax meal, salt, and xanthan gum.

3. In a separate large mixing bowl (or the bowl of a stand mixer), dissolve the yeast in the room temperature water. Add the olive oil and maple syrup. Just as the yeast comes alive and begins to feed on the maple syrup, add the combined dry ingredients and the chia seeds with their soaking liquid. Combine well to the point that you have a lovely, pliable bread dough. Because my bread doughs are wetter than traditional bread doughs you may be surprised at how quickly the

dough comes together. Mix thoroughly only until the dough holds together; do not continue mixing the dough. Go ahead and use your stand mixer with a paddle pulsed on low speed, or if you prefer to use your arm and a wooden spoon, by all means enjoy this slightly slower but very effective way of mixing your bread dough!

4. On a work surface generously dusted with brown rice flour or teff flour, turn out the dough and divide into 2 equal portions. Gently form each piece into a baton shape about the length of your sheet pan. I suggest beginning to roll out the baton on the counter and then transferring it to the prepared baking sheet where you can finish elongating the dough. Score with parallel ¼-inch-deep diagonal lines across the batons, about 3 inches apart. Sprinkle with coarse sea salt. Bake for 1 hour and 30 minutes, until golden brown and crusty.

✦ Grissini ✦

Grissini are delightfully addictive Italian bread sticks, often found on the tables of informal Italian restaurants. Strikingly elongated in shape, they are so versatile; you can add various herbs, spices, or seeds (paprika, cumin, rosemary, thyme, and sesame or poppy seeds, just to name a few possibilities). They are alarmingly tasty and their baking time is quite short. This recipe is a joy to make with kids, who are sure to have a lot of fun rolling out the dough and sprinkling on the seeds. It also makes for two exceptional baguettes, should you want to play around with the dough. For baguettes, follow the shaping and baking instructions in the Multiple Grain Baguette recipe (page 32). Gustare!

⟨⟨⟨⟨⟨⟨⟨⟨⟨⟨⟨⟨⟨⟨⟨⟨⟨⟨⟨⟨ **MAKES 14 BREAD STICKS** ⟩⟩⟩⟩⟩⟩⟩⟩⟩⟩⟩⟩⟩⟩⟩⟩⟩⟩⟩⟩

2 tablespoons chia seeds

½ cup water

1 cup tapioca flour

½ cup arrowroot

½ cup garbanzo bean flour

½ cup teff flour

½ cup sorghum flour

½ cup brown rice flour

¼ cup flax meal

1 teaspoon sea salt, plus additional for sprinkling

1 teaspoon xanthan gum

1 envelope (2¾ teaspoons) active dry yeast

1½ cups room temperature filtered water

3 tablespoons canola oil

2 tablespoons evaporated cane juice

Sesame or poppy seeds, for sprinkling

1. Soak the chia seeds in the ½ cup water for at least 15 minutes. Preheat the oven to 425 degrees F and place a water bath on the bottom rack or the oven floor. Line 2 sheet pans with parchment paper.

2. In a large mixing bowl, combine the tapioca flour, arrowroot, garbanzo bean flour, teff flour, sorghum flour, brown rice flour, flax meal, salt, and xanthan gum.

3. In a separate large mixing bowl (or the bowl of a stand mixer), dissolve the yeast in the room temperature water. Add the canola oil and evaporated cane juice. Just as the yeast begins to foam and feed on the cane juice, add the combined dry ingredients and the chia seeds with their soaking liquid. Mix until a soft dough forms. You can do this by hand with a strong arm and a sturdy spoon, or with your stand mixer and the paddle attachment pulsed on low speed.

4. On a work surface generously dusted with brown rice flour, turn out the soft dough and divide into 14 pieces. Roll each piece of dough to the length of your sheet pan. I suggest beginning to roll out each snake-like shape on the counter and then transferring it to the prepared baking sheet to finish elongating, as it is more challenging to transfer the dough the skinnier and longer the snake becomes! You can just roll the dough back and forth on the sheet pan without using up much space at all. It works well to bake 7 bread sticks per sheet pan to allow for extra room for shaping each one. Brush each unbaked bread stick with a pastry brush dipped in water. Sprinkle with sesame or poppy seeds and sea salt. Bake for 35 minutes, until golden.

✦ Soft Millet Sandwich Bread ✦

A mellow-flavored, soft sandwich bread with a perfect golden crust, this loaf reminds me of the white bread I would long for as a child. Growing up, all of our starches were whole grain and I pined for the white bread sandwiches I saw other children eating. Of course, now I am extremely grateful for the healthy choices my parents made, but I still do sometimes crave white bread–type sandwiches, and this loaf satisfies that craving while still being very nutritious. Being so light, the bread is a wonderful loaf to serve your children. The arrowroot is full of calcium, and the millet, quinoa, and brown rice flours are full of fiber, protein, and nutrients. The flax meal provides additional fiber, as do the super chia seeds. So enjoy wholeheartedly!

◇◇◇◇◇◇◇◇◇◇◇◇◇◇◇◇◇◇◇◇◇ **MAKES 1 LARGE LOAF** ◇◇◇◇◇◇◇◇◇◇◇◇◇◇◇◇◇◇◇◇◇

2 tablespoons chia seeds

½ cup water

1 cup arrowroot

1 cup millet flour

½ cup quinoa flour

½ brown rice flour

½ cup tapioca flour

⅓ cup flax meal

1 teaspoon sea salt

1 teaspoon xanthan gum

1 envelope (2¾ teaspoons) active dry yeast

1½ cups room temperature filtered water

3 tablespoons olive oil

2 tablespoons maple syrup

2 teaspoons sesame seeds, for sprinkling

1. Soak the chia seeds in the ½ cup water for at least 15 minutes. Preheat the oven to 425 degrees F. Lightly grease an 8-by-4-by-4-inch loaf pan and dust with brown rice flour.

2. In a large mixing bowl, combine the arrowroot, millet flour, quinoa flour, brown rice flour, tapioca flour, flax meal, salt, and xanthan gum.

3. In a separate large mixing bowl (or the bowl of a stand mixer), dissolve the yeast in the room temperature water. Add the olive oil and maple syrup. Just as the yeast begins to foam and feed on the maple syrup, about 3 minutes, add

the combined dry ingredients and the chia seeds with their soaking liquid. Mix until you have achieved a soft dough. This will not take long. A stand mixer with a paddle attachment works well, but so will an old-fashioned wooden spoon and a tireless arm.

4. Once your dough is formed, use a spatula to guide and pour the batter-like dough into the prepared loaf pan. Smooth the surface so that it is even and attractive. Sprinkle with the sesame seeds and score with one line that runs the length of the dough, just off center. Place in the hot oven. Once the door of the oven is closed, decrease the temperature to 350 degrees F and bake for 1 hour and 45 minutes, until golden brown and crusty.

✦ Quinoa Sandwich Bread ✦

Quinoa, referred to as "the mother of all grains" by the Incas, is rich in protein and amino acids, including lysine, which can be challenging to find in vegetarian sources. This nourishing sandwich loaf is mild in flavor, but distinguishes itself from the other sandwich breads in this book by the unique essence of quinoa.

×××××××××××××××××××××××××××× **MAKES 1 LARGE LOAF** ××××××××××××××××××××××××××××

2 tablespoons chia seeds

½ cup water

1 cup millet flour

1 cup quinoa flour

1 cup tapioca flour

½ cup almond meal

½ cup arrowroot

¼ cup flax meal

1 teaspoon sea salt

1 teaspoon xanthan gum

1 envelope (2¾ teaspoons) active dry yeast

1½ cups room temperature filtered water

3 tablespoons canola oil

2 tablespoons maple syrup

1 tablespoon sesame seeds, for sprinkling (optional)

1. Soak the chia seeds in the ½ cup water for at least 15 minutes. Preheat the oven to 425 degrees F. Lightly grease and flour an 8-by-4-by-4-inch loaf pan.

2. In a large mixing bowl, combine the millet flour, quinoa flour, tapioca flour, almond meal, arrowroot, flax meal, salt, and xanthan gum.

3. In a separate large mixing bowl (or the mixing bowl of a stand mixer), dissolve the yeast in the room temperature water. Add the canola oil and maple syrup. Just as the yeast begins to foam and feed on the maple syrup, about 3 minutes, add the combined dry ingredients and the chia seeds with their soaking liquid. Mix thoroughly, just until the dough holds together. This will take just a few moments. You can do this by hand with a strong arm and a sturdy spoon, or with your stand mixer and the paddle attachment pulsed on low speed.

4. Once your dough is formed, use a spatula to guide and pour the batter-like dough into the prepared loaf pan. Smooth the surface so that it is even and attractive. Sprinkle with the sesame seeds and score with one line that runs the length of the dough, just off center. Place the loaf in the hot oven. Once the door of the oven is closed, decrease the temperature to 350 degrees F and bake for 2 hours and 30 minutes, until golden brown and crusty.

✦ Light Teff Sandwich Bread ✦

This sandwich bread differs from the other sandwich breads in this chapter by utilizing the wonderfully wholesome teff flour, which contributes a slightly nutty taste and darker color. It's a scrumptious loaf that is reminiscent of soft wheat sandwich breads made with a combination of white flour and whole wheat flour.

⬦⬦⬦⬦⬦⬦⬦⬦⬦⬦⬦⬦⬦⬦⬦⬦⬦⬦⬦⬦⬦ **MAKES 1 LARGE LOAF** ⬦⬦⬦⬦⬦⬦⬦⬦⬦⬦⬦⬦⬦⬦⬦⬦⬦⬦⬦⬦⬦

2 tablespoons chia seeds

½ cup water

1 cup arrowroot

1 cup millet flour

¾ cup teff flour

½ cup almond meal

½ cup tapioca flour

⅓ cup flax meal

1 teaspoon sea salt

1 teaspoon xanthan gum

1 envelope (2¾ teaspoons) active dry yeast

1½ cups room temperature filtered water

3 tablespoons olive oil

2 tablespoons maple syrup

Poppy seeds, for sprinkling

1. Soak the chia seeds in the ½ cup water for at least 15 minutes. Preheat the oven to 425 degrees F. Lightly grease an 8-by-4-by-4-inch loaf pan and dust with brown rice flour.

2. In a large mixing bowl, combine the arrowroot, millet flour, teff flour, almond meal, tapioca flour, flax meal, salt, and xanthan gum.

3. In a separate large mixing bowl (or the mixing bowl of a stand mixer), dissolve the yeast in the room temperature water. Add the olive oil and maple syrup. Just as the yeast begins to foam and feed on the maple syrup, about 3 minutes, add the combined dry ingredients and the chia seeds with their soaking liquid. Mix just until a soft dough forms. You can do this by hand with a strong arm and a sturdy spoon, or with your stand mixer and the paddle attachment pulsed on low speed.

4. Once the dough is formed (it won't take long), use a spatula to guide and pour the batter-like dough into the prepared loaf pan. Smooth the surface so that it is even and attractive. Sprinkle with the poppy seeds and score with one line that runs the length of the dough, just off center. Place the loaf in the hot oven. Once the door of the oven is closed, decrease the temperature to 350 degrees F and bake for 1 hour and 45 minutes, until golden brown and crusty.

✦ Cinnamon-Walnut Loaf ✦

It could be argued that cinnamon-walnut bread is the ultimate breakfast pleaser. A warm piece of cinnamon toast slathered with nut butter is indeed a very enjoyable way to greet the day. Not as sweet, of course, as the related cinnamon roll (see pages 63 and 65), but more sustaining and equally delicious in a less sacchariferous manner. If you're feeling adventurous, toast the bread and use it as the base of an open face sandwich piled high with greens, curried hummus, heirloom tomato slices, and a bit of avocado, all drizzled with walnut oil and a smidgen of sea salt.

◇◇◇◇◇◇◇◇◇◇◇◇◇◇◇◇◇◇◇◇◇ **MAKES 1 LARGE LOAF** ◇◇◇◇◇◇◇◇◇◇◇◇◇◇◇◇◇◇◇◇◇

2 tablespoons chia seeds

½ cup water

1 cup arrowroot

1 cup millet flour

1 cup teff flour

⅓ cup flax meal

¼ cup tapioca flour

¼ cup potato starch

1 teaspoon cinnamon

1 teaspoon sea salt

1 teaspoon xanthan gum

1 cup walnuts, finely chopped

½ cup dark or golden raisins

1 envelope (2¾ teaspoons) active dry yeast

1½ cups room temperature filtered water

3 tablespoons olive oil

3 tablespoons maple syrup

1. Soak the chia seeds in the ½ cup water for at least 15 minutes. Preheat the oven to 425 degrees F. Lightly grease an 8-by-4-by-4-inch loaf pan and dust with brown rice flour or teff flour.

2. In a large mixing bowl, combine the arrowroot, millet flour, teff flour, flax meal, tapioca flour, potato starch, cinnamon, salt, and xanthan gum. Mix in the walnuts and raisins.

3. In a separate large mixing bowl (or the bowl of a stand mixer), dissolve the yeast in the room temperature water. Add the olive oil and maple syrup. Just as the yeast begins to foam and feed on the maple syrup, about 3 minutes, add

the combined dry ingredients and the chia seeds with their soaking liquid. Mix well, just until the dough is soft and holding together. This will happen sooner than you may expect. If you are using a stand mixer, insert the paddle attachment and pulse on low speed. Otherwise a wooden spoon will certainly do the trick.

4. Once the dough has formed, use a spatula to guide and pour the batter-like dough into the prepared loaf pan. Smooth the surface so that it is even and attractive and score with one line that runs the length of the dough, just off center. Place the loaf in the hot oven. Once the door of the oven is closed, decrease the temperature to 350 degrees F and bake for 2 hours, until golden brown and crusty.

✦ Swedish Braided Bread ✦

This soft, slightly sweet bread will fill your home with a warming cardamom aroma. The bread is a joy to make and even more so to taste. Braided breads are also so much fun to form. Children love to engage in baking and cooking, and helping braid dough is a delight for their senses. I often set a bit of dough aside so that my daughter can shape and form her own little braid to bake. Note that forming the loaf works out most smoothly if you shape and braid the dough directly on the sheet pan. An icing to top the bread is extra decadent should you wish for a sweeter, more festive bread experience (but it is certainly not a necessity): Drizzle the hot baked braid with a simple glaze made of sifted powdered evaporated cane juice whisked with a smidgen of hot water and a drop or two of vanilla extract.

××××××××××××××××××××××××××× **MAKES 1 LARGE LOAF** ×××××××××××××××××××××××××××

2 tablespoons chia seeds

½ cup water

1 cup tapioca flour

¾ cup brown rice flour

½ cup garbanzo bean flour

½ cup millet flour

½ cup almond meal

¼ cup sorghum flour

1 teaspoon sea salt

½ teaspoon ground cardamom

½ teaspoon ground cinnamon

1 teaspoon xanthan gum

1 envelope (2¾ teaspoons) active dry yeast

1 cup room temperature filtered water

3 tablespoons canola oil

2 tablespoons Sucanat

1. Soak the chia seeds in the ½ cup water for at least 15 minutes. Preheat the oven to 350 degrees F. Line a sheet pan with parchment paper.

2. In a large mixing bowl, combine the tapioca flour, brown rice flour, garbanzo bean flour, millet flour, almond meal, sorghum flour, salt, cardamom, cinnamon, and xanthan gum.

3. In a separate large mixing bowl (or the bowl of a stand mixer), dissolve the yeast in the room temperature water. Add the canola oil and Sucanat. Just as the

yeast begins to foam and feed on the Sucanat, about 3 minutes, add the combined dry ingredients and the chia seeds with their soaking liquid. Combine well to the point that you have a lovely, pliable bread dough. If you are using a stand mixer, insert the paddle attachment and pulse on low speed. If you prefer to use your arm and a wooden spoon, by all means enjoy this slightly slower but very effective way of mixing your bread dough!

4. On a work surface generously dusted with brown rice flour, turn out the dough and gently divide into 3 equal pieces. Begin rolling out each piece on the prepared work surface, then transfer ropes-in-progress onto baking sheet pan lined with parchment paper and dusted with brown rice flour. Keep rolling until finished length of each rope measures 12 inches.

5. To braid the ropes together, approach the dough as you would hair. With 3 ropes next to each other on the sheet pan, hold the 2 outer sections, with the left rope in your left hand and the right rope in your right hand; the center rope will be resting on the sheet pan. Lift the left rope over the center rope and set it down so it is between the right rope and the center rope. Then pick up the old center section with your left hand and pull it to the left, creating more space between the ropes for the next move. Now, bring the right section over the center. Repeat the process, alternating sides, until the entire length of bread is braided. Press the ends of the strands together and tuck each end slightly under the loaf. Bake for 1 hour and 30 minutes, until golden brown and crusty.

✦ Orange Chocolate Bread ✦

This sophisticated, rich dark chocolate boule is full of cocoa flavor. When I first made it, I did not include the chopped dark chocolate. It is exceptional both ways, but if you are craving a touch of extra sweetness and some warm dark morsels melting throughout your bread, then by all means incorporate the dark chocolate bits. I prefer anything over 70 percent cacao. Most high-percentage chocolates are vegan, but you may want to double-check. For this recipe I recommend using black chia seeds for purely aesthetic reasons.

◇◇◇◇◇◇◇◇◇◇◇◇◇◇◇◇◇◇◇◇◇◇◇◇ **MAKES 1 MEDIUM LOAF** ◇◇◇◇◇◇◇◇◇◇◇◇◇◇◇◇◇◇◇◇◇◇◇◇

¼ cup black chia seeds

¾ cup water

1½ cups tapioca flour

1 cup sorghum flour

1 cup almond meal

½ cup unsweetened cocoa powder

¼ cup cocoa nibs

¼ cup dark chocolate, finely chopped (optional)

1 teaspoon sea salt

1 teaspoon xanthan gum

½ teaspoon grated orange zest

1 envelope (2¾ teaspoons) active dry yeast

¾ cup room temperature filtered water

¼ cup maple syrup

3 tablespoons extra-virgin olive oil

1. Soak the chia seeds in the ¾ cup water for at least 15 minutes. Preheat the oven to 350 degrees F. Lightly oil a sheet pan and dust with brown rice flour or line with parchment paper.

2. In a large mixing bowl, combine the tapioca flour, sorghum flour, almond meal, cocoa powder, cocoa nibs, chopped chocolate, salt, xanthan gum, and orange zest.

3. In a separate large mixing bowl (or the mixing bowl of a stand mixer), dissolve the yeast in the room temperature water. Add the maple syrup and olive oil. Just as the yeast begins to foam and feed on the maple syrup, about 3 minutes, add the combined dry ingredients and the chia seeds with their soaking liquid.

Mix until a soft dough forms. You can do this by hand with a strong arm and a sturdy spoon, or with your stand mixer and the paddle attachment pulsed on low speed. This dough comes together quickly.

4. With clean dry hands, shape the dough directly on your counter into a round. It is unlikely you will need any extra flour to do so. However, if you find that the dough is sticking a little bit, use a dusting of cocoa powder to help shape it. Place the loaf on the prepared sheet pan. Score the bread with a semicircle shape. Bake for 2 hours and 20 minutes, until firm to the touch with a dark chocolate-colored crust.

✦ Friendship Tea Ring ✦

I fell in love with cardamom rather late in life, but since then I find ways to include the gorgeously aromatic, warming, and softening spice in my recipes. This tea ring is a sweet bread that I adore for numerous reasons. First, it has a balanced, but ever so present, amount of cardamom in both the dough and the filling. I am also quite fond of its special fanned-out ring structure with its lovely contours showing off views of the delicious gooey and nutty filling. Lastly, the soft, sweet bread dough wrapped around the fragrant walnut filling is ever so satisfying—it's a wonderful treat to enjoy with friends.

◇◇◇◇◇◇◇◇◇◇◇◇◇◇◇◇◇◇◇◇ **MAKES 1 MEDIUM TEA RING** ◇◇◇◇◇◇◇◇◇◇◇◇◇◇◇◇◇◇◇◇

WALNUT FILLING

1 cup walnuts

2 tablespoons Sucanat

1½ tablespoons olive oil

1½ teaspoons ground cinnamon

¼ teaspoon ground cardamom

DOUGH

1 cup teff flour, plus ½ cup additional for rolling and shaping

1 cup tapioca flour

½ cup sorghum flour

½ cup millet flour

½ cup flax meal

1 teaspoon sea salt

1 teaspoon xanthan gum

½ teaspoon ground cardamom

1 envelope (2¾ teaspoons) active dry yeast

1½ cups room temperature filtered water

3 tablespoons extra-virgin olive oil

2 tablespoons maple syrup

1. Preheat the oven to 350 degrees F.

2. For the filling, place the walnuts, Sucanat, olive oil, cinnamon, and cardamom in a food processor and pulse until the walnuts are finely ground, but before a butter-like paste forms. If you do not have a food processor, simply finely chop the walnuts and combine with the other filling ingredients in a small bowl.

3. To make the dough, combine the teff flour, tapioca flour, sorghum flour, millet flour, flax meal, sea salt, xanthan gum, and cardamom in a large mixing bowl.

4. In another large mixing bowl (or the bowl of a stand mixer), dissolve the yeast in the room temperature water. Add the olive oil and maple syrup. Just as the yeast begins to foam and feed on the maple syrup, about 3 minutes, add the combined dry ingredients. Mix thoroughly but just until the dough holds together. This will take just a few moments. You can do this by hand with a strong arm and a sturdy spoon, or with your stand mixer and the paddle attachment pulsed on low speed.

5. Turn the dough out onto a sheet of parchment paper at least 16 inches long that is generously dusted with the teff flour. With floured clean hands, gently spread the dough into a rectangle that is 16 inches long and 10 inches wide. Spread the filling over the flattened dough, evenly coating the rectangle.

6. Now for rolling up! Turn the paper so that the long side of the rectangle is nearest you. Begin rolling, using the parchment to lift the dough and roll it over onto itself. The parchment is a great aid in allowing you to roll up the dough with ease, gracefully turning the rectangle into a snug cylinder.

7. Transfer the cylinder to the prepared baking pan with the help of the parchment paper: Simply pick up the parchment paper while supporting the dough and set them both right on the sheet pan. Bring the 2 ends together and form a ring; pinch the ends together. Around the ring, make 10 equally spaced indentations to indicate where to cut. With scissors, make cuts that go from the outside inward, but not quite all the way through. Gently pull the sections away from the ring at an angle, creating a beautiful wreath. Bake the ring for 1 hour and 35 minutes, until golden brown and crusty.

✦ Sweet Perrin ✦

There is an exceptional bakery in Seattle that specializes in a wide variety of artisan breads. Every autumn I welcome the arrival of Essential Baking Company's Sweet Perrin (pear bread). Here, I take on the challenge of creating a gluten-free and vegan version. I must say I am thrilled with the outcome! Bon appétit!

ᐉᐉᐉᐉᐉᐉᐉᐉᐉᐉᐉᐉᐉᐉᐉᐉᐉᐉ **MAKES 1 LARGE LOAF** ᐊᐊᐊᐊᐊᐊᐊᐊᐊᐊᐊᐊᐊᐊᐊᐊᐊᐊ

2 tablespoons chia seeds

½ cup water

1¼ cups teff flour

1 cup arrowroot

½ cup almond meal

¼ cup flax meal

1 teaspoon sea salt

½ teaspoon ground cinnamon

½ teaspoon xanthan gum

1 pear, peeled, cored, and finely chopped

½ cup pecans, finely chopped

1½ teaspoons active dry yeast

¾ cup room temperature filtered water

2 tablespoons olive oil

2 tablespoons maple syrup

1. Soak the chia seeds in the ½ cup water for at least 15 minutes. Preheat the oven to 425 degrees F.

2. In a large mixing bowl, combine the teff flour, arrowroot, almond meal, flax meal, salt, cinnamon, and xanthan gum. Add the pear and pecans and toss gently.

3. In a separate large mixing bowl (or the bowl of a stand mixer), dissolve the yeast in the room temperature water. Add the olive oil and maple syrup. Just as the yeast begins to foam and feed on the maple syrup, about 3 minutes, add the combined dry ingredients and the chia seeds with their soaking liquid. Mix until you have achieved a soft dough. This will not take long. A stand mixer with a paddle attachment works well, but so will an old-fashioned wooden spoon and a tireless arm.

4. On a work surface generously dusted with teff flour, turn out the dough and gently form into a batard shape. Score with one line that runs the length of the batard, just off center. Place shaped dough in the hot oven. After the oven door has closed, decrease the temperature to 350 degrees F and bake for 2 hours and 45 minutes, until golden brown and crusty.

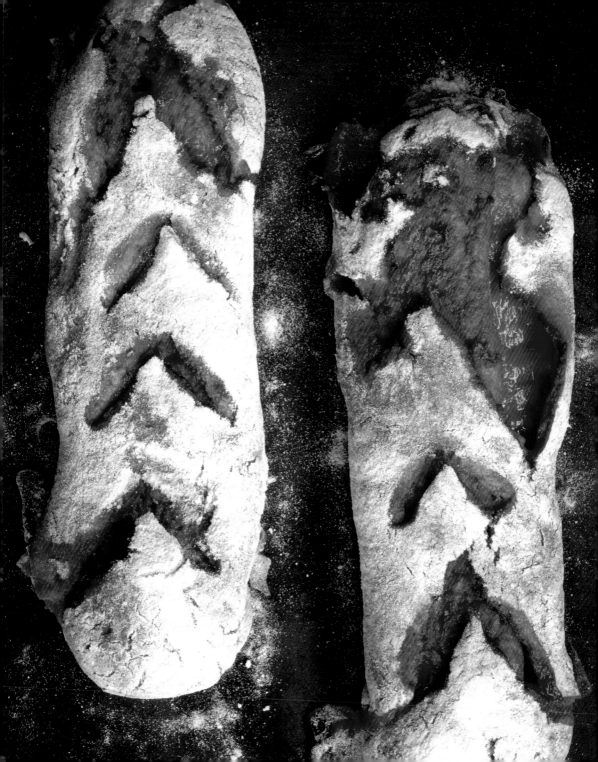

✦ Apricot Kuchen ✦

This recipe is in honor of my grandmother Colletta, who made the most amazing apricot kuchens every time she visited—a cherished family tradition. I believe she would really enjoy a piece of this gluten-free vegan version with a piping hot cup of coffee. This recipe makes two kuchens but is easily halved to make one. A store-bought apricot jam is a delicious substitute for the filling if you have limited time. But at some point, do make the homemade apricot filling, as it is heavenly! If you are making your own filling, be sure to give the apricots a two-hour head start for soaking. You'll have extra—it keeps well, refrigerated in a tightly sealed container. It is spectacular on toast!

◇◇◇◇◇◇◇◇◇◇◇◇◇◇◇◇◇ **MAKES 2 MEDIUM KUCHENS** ◇◇◇◇◇◇◇◇◇◇◇◇◇◇◇◇◇

APRICOT FILLING

1½ cups dried apricots

2 cups boiling water

1½ tablespoons organic whole cane sugar (optional)

1 tablespoon freshly squeezed lemon juice

2 teaspoons vanilla extract

DOUGH

1½ cups sorghum flour

1½ cups tapioca flour

¾ cup brown rice flour

½ cup almond meal

½ cup flax meal

1 teaspoon sea salt

1 teaspoon xanthan gum

1 tablespoon active dry yeast

1½ cups room temperature filtered water

¼ cup maple syrup

3 tablespoons extra-virgin olive oil

Vanilla frosting or sifted powdered evaporated cane juice (optional)

1. To make the filling, in a large bowl, soak the dried apricots in the boiling water, covered, for 2 hours. Drain the apricots, reserving ¼ cup of the soaking liquid. (Do go ahead and reserve all of it for a sweet drink if you wish!) Transfer the apricots and reserved soaking liquid to a food processor or blender and purée until smooth. Blend in the cane sugar, lemon juice, and vanilla.

2. To make the dough, preheat the oven to 350 degrees F. In a large mixing bowl, combine the sorghum flour, tapioca flour, brown rice flour, almond meal, flax meal, salt, and xanthan gum.

3. In another large mixing bowl (or the bowl of a stand mixer), dissolve the yeast in the room temperature water. Add the maple syrup and olive oil. Just as the yeast begins to foam and feed on the maple syrup, about 3 minutes, add the combined dry ingredients and mix just until a soft dough forms. You can do this by hand with a strong arm and a sturdy spoon, or with your stand mixer and the paddle attachment pulsed on low speed.

4. Turn the dough out onto the counter and divide into 2 equal portions. Generously dust a sheet of parchment paper that is at least 12 inches long with brown rice flour. With floured clean hands, gently shape 1 portion of the dough on the parchment paper into a rectangle that is 12 inches long and 10 inches wide. Spread half (about ¾ cup) of the filling over the dough, evenly coating the surface.

5. Now for rolling up! Turn the paper so that the long side of the rectangle is nearest you. Begin rolling, using the parchment to lift the dough and roll it over onto itself. The parchment is a great aid in allowing you to roll up the dough with ease, gracefully turning the rectangle into a snug cylinder. Transfer the cylinder to the prepared baking pan with the help of the parchment paper: Simply pick up the parchment paper while supporting the dough and set them both right on the sheet pan. (You can keep the parchment paper underneath your dough while baking.) Repeat with the second portion of dough.

6. Next comes the really artful and exciting part! With a pair of clean scissors, make 3 or 4 incisions on top of each cylinder. Approach the dough at a 45-degree angle and make cuts like the letter V. Be sure to start your incisions at least 2 inches in from each end, and space them evenly. Bake for 1 hour and 50 minutes, until golden brown and crusty. When cooled, frost with vanilla frosting or dust with sifted powdered evaporated cane juice.

✦ Saint Lucia Buns ✦

Saint Lucia buns are a delicious Swedish tradition that are enjoyed every December. There is a beautiful legend about a young woman named Lucia (which means "light" in Swedish) who, with a wreath of candles adorning her head so that she could see through the dark of the night, sneakily carried bread to people in need. The buns made in honor of Saint Lucia are often shaped in a circle signifying a crown, or in S-shaped swirls. These soft buns are ever so lightly sweetened and make for a warming breakfast treat. For an extra sweet experience, drizzle the hot buns with a simple glaze made of sifted powdered evaporated cane juice whisked with a smidgen of orange juice or hot water and a drop or two of vanilla extract.

◇◇◇◇◇◇◇◇◇◇◇◇◇◇◇◇◇◇◇◇◇ **MAKES 8 BUNS** ◇◇◇◇◇◇◇◇◇◇◇◇◇◇◇◇◇◇◇◇◇

2 tablespoons chia seeds

½ cup water

2 cups teff flour

1 cup arrowroot

½ cup tapioca flour

¼ cup flax meal

1 teaspoon saffron threads, finely chopped and dissolved in a few drops of water

1 teaspoon ground cinnamon

1 teaspoon sea salt

1 teaspoon xanthan gum

½ cup currants

1 envelope (2¾ teaspoons) active dry yeast

1½ cups room temperature filtered water

3 tablespoons olive oil

2 tablespoons maple syrup

1. Soak the chia seeds in the ½ cup water for at least 15 minutes. Preheat the oven to 350 degrees F. Lightly grease a sheet pan or line with parchment paper.

2. In a large mixing bowl, combine the teff flour, arrowroot, tapioca flour, flax meal, saffron, cinnamon, salt, and xanthan gum. Mix in the currants.

3. In a separate large mixing bowl (or the bowl of a stand mixer), dissolve the yeast in the room temperature water. Add the olive oil and maple syrup. Just as the yeast begins to foam and feed on the maple syrup, about 3 minutes, add the

combined dry ingredients and the chia seeds with their soaking liquid. Mix well just until the dough is soft and holding together. This will happen sooner than you may expect. You can do this by hand with a strong arm and a sturdy spoon, or with your stand mixer and the paddle attachment pulsed on low speed.

4. On a work surface generously dusted with brown rice flour or teff flour, turn out the dough and gently divide into 8 equal pieces. There are a couple of fun shape options for these buns. One is the simple hot cross bun we all know. Another is an S shape made by rolling out a 4- to 5-inch-long fat snake and curling it into an S. You can also roll out a somewhat longer snake and coil it into a tight, snail-like swirl. Place the shaped buns on the prepared sheet pan and bake for 1 hour and 10 minutes, until golden and slightly firm to the touch. If you are finishing with the glaze (see headnote), wait until the bread has dooled before drizzling.

✦ Czech Easter Wreath ✦

The Czech Easter Wreath is a celebratory loaf, traditionally enjoyed after a long fast. I find it to be a fantastic bread to wow brunch guests with. The sweet yeasty bread is so soft and luscious, and the shape is quite festive. And who can resist the little bits of dried red cherries and orange zest peeking through the light bread, topped with a shimmery glaze of creamy frosting? To make the frosting, whisk sifted powdered evaporated cane juice with a smidgen of orange juice or hot water and a drop of vanilla.

◇◇◇◇◇◇◇◇◇◇◇◇◇◇◇◇◇◇◇◇◇◇ **MAKES 1 MEDIUM LOAF** ◇◇◇◇◇◇◇◇◇◇◇◇◇◇◇◇◇◇◇◇◇◇

2 tablespoons chia seeds

½ cup water

1 cup brown rice flour

1 cup tapioca flour

½ cup garbanzo bean flour

½ cup millet flour

½ cup almond meal

1 teaspoon sea salt

1 teaspoon xanthan gum

½ cup dried cherries

⅓ cup slivered almonds, plus additional 2 tablespoons for sprinkling

½ teaspoon grated orange zest

1 envelope (2¾ teaspoons) active dry yeast

1 cup room temperature filtered water

3 tablespoons canola oil

2 tablespoons maple syrup

1. Soak the chia seeds in the ½ cup water for at least 15 minutes. Preheat the oven to 350 degrees F. Lightly grease a sheet pan or line with parchment paper.

2. In a large mixing bowl, combine the brown rice flour, tapioca flour, garbanzo bean flour, millet flour, almond meal, salt, and xanthan gum. Mix in the dried cherries, ⅓ cup slivered almonds, and orange zest.

3. In a separate large mixing bowl (or the mixing bowl of a stand mixer), dissolve the yeast in the room temperature water. Add the canola oil and maple syrup. Just as the yeast begins to foam and feed on the maple syrup, about 3 minutes, add the combined dry ingredients and the chia seeds with their soaking liquid.

(Because my bread doughs are wetter than traditional bread doughs you may be surprised at how quickly the dough comes together.) Mix thoroughly until the dough holds together and becomes a lovely, pliable bread dough—at which point please do not continue mixing the dough. You can do this by hand with a strong arm and a sturdy spoon, or with your stand mixer and the paddle attachment pulsed on low speed.

4. On a work surface generously dusted with brown rice flour, turn out the dough and divide into 8 equal pieces. Gently shape into round rolls and arrange in a tight circular wreath, snuggling next to each other, on the prepared sheet pan. Sprinkle with the 2 tablespoons slivered almonds and bake for 1 hour and 20 minutes, until golden and slightly firm to the touch. Wait until the bread has cooled before adding the frosting.

✦ Pecan Cinnamon Rolls ✦

Here we have gorgeous cinnamon rolls for all those who fancy the delicate and buttery taste of pecans! They are a more affordable option than my Raisin Cinnamon Rolls (page 65), which call for maple butter. They come together in much the same fashion and are equally scrumptious!

◇◇◇◇◇◇◇◇◇◇◇◇◇◇◇◇◇◇◇◇◇ **MAKES 10 ROLLS** ◇◇◇◇◇◇◇◇◇◇◇◇◇◇◇◇◇◇◇◇◇

FILLING

½ cup pecans

2 tablespoons Sucanat

1 tablespoon canola oil

1 teaspoon ground cinnamon

DOUGH

1 cup sorghum flour

1 cup tapioca flour

½ cup brown rice flour

½ cup garbanzo bean flour

½ cup millet flour

½ cup flax meal

1 teaspoon sea salt

1 teaspoon xanthan gum

½ teaspoon ground cinnamon

1 envelope (2¾ teaspoons) active dry yeast

1½ cups room temperature filtered water

3 tablespoons extra-virgin olive oil

2 tablespoons Sucanat

1. Preheat the oven to 350 degrees F. Lightly grease a 9-inch cake or pie pan.

2. To make the filling, place the pecans, Sucanat, canola oil, and cinnamon in a food processor and pulse until the pecans are finely ground, but not so much that a butter-like paste forms. If you do not have a food processor, simply finely chop the pecans and combine with the other filling ingredients in a small bowl.

3. To make the dough, in a large mixing bowl, combine the sorghum flour, tapioca flour, brown rice flour, garbanzo bean flour, millet flour, flax meal, salt, xanthan gum, and cinnamon.

4. In another large mixing bowl (or the bowl of a stand mixer), dissolve the yeast in the room temperature water. Add the olive oil and Sucanat. Just as the yeast begins to foam and feed on the Sucanat, about 3 minutes, add the combined dry ingredients. Mix until a soft dough forms. You can do this by hand with a strong arm and a sturdy spoon, or with your stand mixer and the paddle attachment pulsed on low speed. The dough comes together quickly.

5. Generously dust a sheet of parchment paper that is at least 16 inches long with brown rice flour. Turn the dough out onto the parchment paper and with floured clean hands, gently spread into a rectangle that is 16 inches long and 10 inches wide. Spread the filling over the flattened dough, evenly coating the surface.

6. Now for rolling up! Turn the paper so that the long side of the rectangle is nearest you. Begin rolling, using the parchment to lift the dough and roll it over onto itself. The parchment is a great aid in allowing you to roll up the dough with ease, gracefully turning the rectangle into a snug cylinder.

7. Measure out 1½-inch sections and slice the cylinder into 10 pieces. Place the slices close together in the prepared cake or pie pan and bake for 1 hour and 10 minutes, until golden and slightly firm to the touch.

✦ Raisin Cinnamon Rolls ✦

Cinnamon rolls are the ultimate winter-morning comfort food! These are especially delicious because of the rich, caramel-like maple butter filling! Although the maple butter does cost a pretty penny, the flavor is extraordinary and leaves you feeling satisfied without a sugar crash.

2 tablespoons chia seeds

½ cup water

1 cup brown rice flour

1 cup tapioca flour

½ cup garbanzo bean flour

½ cup millet flour

½ cup almond meal

1 teaspoon sea salt

1 teaspoon xanthan gum

1½ teaspoons ground cinnamon

1 envelope (2¾ teaspoons) active dry yeast

1 cup room temperature filtered water

3 tablespoons extra-virgin olive oil

2 tablespoons maple syrup

½ cup maple butter

½ cup dark or golden raisins, soaked in 1 cup boiling water for 20 minutes, drained

1. Soak the chia seeds in the ½ cup water for at least 15 minutes. Preheat the oven to 350 degrees F. Lightly grease a 9-inch cake or pie pan.

2. In a large mixing bowl, combine the brown rice flour, tapioca flour, garbanzo bean flour, millet flour, almond meal, salt, xanthan gum, and ½ teaspoon of the cinnamon.

3. In another large mixing bowl (or the bowl of a stand mixer), dissolve the yeast in the room temperature water. Add the olive oil and maple syrup. Just as the yeast begins to foam and feed on the maple syrup, about 3 minutes, add the combined dry ingredients and the chia seeds with their soaking liquid. Mix thoroughly but just until the dough holds together. This will take just a few

moments. You can do this by hand with a strong arm and a sturdy spoon, or in your stand mixer with the paddle attachment pulsed on low speed.

4. Generously dust a sheet of parchment paper that is at least 16 inches long with brown rice flour. Turn the dough out onto the parchment paper and with floured clean hands, gently spread into a rectangle that is 16 inches long and 10 inches wide. Spread the maple butter evenly over the dough, and follow with the plumped raisins distributed equally. Lastly, sprinkle the remaining 1 teaspoon cinnamon evenly over the maple butter-and-raisin filling.

5. Now for rolling up the dough! Turn the paper so that the long side of the rectangle is nearest you. Begin rolling, using the parchment to lift the dough and roll it over onto itself. The parchment is a great aid in allowing you to roll up the dough with ease, gracefully turning the rectangle into a snug cylinder. Measure out 1½-inch sections and slice into 10 pieces. Place the slices close together in the prepared cake or pie pan. Bake for 1 hour and 10 minutes, until golden and slightly firm to the touch.

✦ Pannetone ✦

Pannetone, which comes from Milan, Italy, is a strikingly puffy loaf of bread that reminds me of a top hat. Traditional pannetone rises three times over 20 hours, the fermentation and leavening adding a distinctive slightly sourdough taste to the bread. To give the bread a subtle touch of that sourdough flavor, I add a very small amount of wild starter to the dough. This is optional, and either way the outcome of the bread is an accomplishment of culinary delight. For a sweet and decorative look, dust the bread with powdered evaporated cane juice after baking.

◇◇◇◇◇◇◇◇◇◇◇◇◇◇◇◇◇◇◇◇◇◇◇◇◇ **MAKES 1 MEDIUM LOAF** ◇◇◇◇◇◇◇◇◇◇◇◇◇◇◇◇◇◇◇◇◇◇◇◇◇

1 cup brown rice flour

1 cup tapioca flour

½ cup garbanzo bean flour

½ cup millet flour

½ cup flax meal flour

1 teaspoon sea salt

1 teaspoon xanthan gum

¼ cup dried blueberries

¼ dried cherries

¼ cup chopped dried papaya or candied citrus

½ teaspoon grated orange zest

1 envelope (2¾ teaspoons) active dry yeast

1½ teaspoons Mother Wild Starter (p. 79), optional

1½ cups room temperature filtered water

3 tablespoons olive oil

3 tablespoons Sucanat

1. Preheat the oven to 350 degrees F. Lightly grease a 6-inch cake pan and dust with brown rice flour.

2. In a large mixing bowl, combine the brown rice flour, tapioca flour, garbanzo bean flour, millet flour, flax meal, salt, and xanthan gum. Combine the dried blueberries, cherries, papaya, and orange zest in a separate small bowl.

3. In another large mixing bowl (or the bowl of a stand mixer), dissolve the yeast and wild starter in the room temperature water. Add the olive oil and Sucanat.

Just as the yeast begins to foam and feed on the Sucanat, about 3 minutes, add the combined dry ingredients and the dried fruit mixture. Mix until you have achieved a soft dough. This will not take long. You can do this by hand with a strong arm and a sturdy spoon, or with your stand mixer and the paddle attachment pulsed on low speed.

4. Turn the dough out onto a work surface dusted with brown rice flour and gently shape into a soft round. Place in the prepared cake pan and score with a semicircle. Bake for 1 hour and 30 minutes on the middle rack of the oven, until golden and firm to the touch.

WILD
STARTER
BREADS

WHEN I BEGAN VISUALIZING THIS COOKBOOK, I knew at the get-go it would be essential to include breads that are leavened with a wild starter. I have met many people who feel intimidated by the mere idea of working with a wild starter, and I must admit that writing this chapter was a bit daunting. But I came away from it with a great sense of ease and confidence, along with the many recipes that follow. So I implore you to put aside any hesitancies and baking insecurities and jump into this marvelous adventure that just might prove to be easier than you expect.

Once you make your wild yeast starter and are in a feeding rhythm, taking care to nurture her with a little extra flour and water twice a week, you will be engaged in an ancient and more intimate tradition of baking. The unique and complex flavors that your wild starter imbues to your breads are extremely gratifying.

When making a wild starter you are actually capturing some of the yeast in the air around you. The starter serves as a habitat, if you will, for microorganisms/yeasts to flourish. In this habitat, through the yeasts' eating, wastes, and reproduction, we bakers will relish in the byproducts from their lives' work. These byproducts being alcohol, carbon dioxide, and acid, which leaven and flavor the bread. I wonder what unique yeasts from your very own kitchen will become a part of the breads you make, and what slight nuance of flavors those specific yeasts will impart!

For research, I spent a great deal of time reading the works of two bread experts, Andrew Whitley and Peter Reinhart. I also found some very educational material at the Wild Yeast Bakery website (www.wildyeastbakery.co.uk). One of the main points I gleaned was the great nutritional value a wild starter brings to breads. There are beneficial bacteria in wild starters that nurture our intestinal tracts by helping to balance the gut flora. This is truly valuable to many of us, especially to those who have recently been diagnosed with celiac disease and are "rebuilding" a healthy intestinal tract. One of the most influential favorable bacteria, *lactobacillus*, propagates in wild starters and is quite prevalent in breads made from them. *Lactobacilli* also create acids that inhibit the growth of unhealthy organisms. As the starter becomes more acidic, the wild strains of yeast live happily, whereas store-bought single-strain yeasts in the same environment perish over time. Also, wild yeasts are less concentrated in their environment than commercial single-strain yeasts (*Saccharomyces cerevisiae*), and their action is much more docile and mellow. Perhaps the variety of the more mild-mannered wild yeasts contributes to the easy digestibility of sourdough breads, comparable to the digestibility of fruit. Another positive aspect is the high level of B-vitamins and biotin found in wild starters.

There is another interesting property of my wild starter. When I first began developing the breads made with the starter, I noticed that in most cases there was no need for xanthan gum. The omission of this ingredient feels quite natural. These breads are full of integrity, depending simply on gluten-free flours, oil, maple syrup, and a few cabbage leaves and a little bit of apple skin to yield a wholesome loaf of bread.

Xanthan gum is used in gluten-free baking as a replacement for gluten. It certainly yields reliable results when added to bread doughs, providing elasticity, structure, and the ability to trap yeast gases. A long chain of three different forms of sugars, it is created (in most cases) when *Xanthomonas campestris* bacteria eat corn sugar and convert it into the ingredient/byproduct we call xanthan gum. What bothers me personally is that the vast majority of xanthan gum is made from genetically modified corn, and also that people with corn allergies might be sensitive to this ingredient. (In addition, some xanthan gum is made from wheat, so it is very important to know your source if you have celiac disease and are on the lookout for trace amounts of gluten.) Also, I have come across numerous cases of people with similar sensitivities to xanthan gum as they have to gluten, such as severe bloating and discomfort. Of course, there could be a number of reasons for this and I do not feel qualified to elaborate; indeed, there are many who have no side effects or allergies to xanthan gum. But my preference is to avoid xanthan gum when possible.

Either way, there is a fascinating coincidence behind an alternative to xanthan gum in wild starter breads. It turns out that xanthan gum is produced naturally on cabbage leaves! Here lies the miraculous coincidence: As I baked breads with my wild starter (made with cabbage leaves but without xanthan gum) and then contemplated the results on walks with Lilli and Joseph, I wondered (not being a scientist) what actually was occurring. Knowing xanthan gum was a digested bacterial byproduct, I surmised that there must be other bacteria in the starter making a substance similar to xanthan gum. It was later that I stumbled across a xanthan gum made by a company named CP Kelco, which advertised their product as being identical to the naturally occurring xanthan gum found on cabbage leaves. What a revelation! Yes, the naturally occurring polysaccharide made by *Xanthomonas campestris* lives on plants belonging to the cabbage family. I cannot say with certainty that xanthan gum is being produced in my starter, but I am most delighted that the properties xanthan gum lends, such as elasticity, suppleness, and the ability to trap gases, are present in my very own wild starter.

(Please note that the loaves in this chapter are beautiful; they have a more crackly exterior crust appearance due to the absence of xanthan gum, yet their internal structures and textures are superb. If you prefer the look of a smooth exterior and are very comfortable with xanthan gum, then feel free to add no more than 1 teaspoon to the wild starter recipes here.)

A quick word and explanation on leavening before jumping into the tips and recipes. In the introduction to the yeasted breads chapter, I write at length

as to why the breads in this cookbook are not left to rise on the counter, but rather go directly into the oven for an accelerated rise, called *oven spring*. The same is true in the case of my wild starter breads, due to the effects of the enzyme protease. It is fast at work breaking down the gluten-free grains. In fact, since protease is perpetually at work on my wild starter (even as it is stored in the fridge), it is important to feed the starter more frequently than for starters made from gluten flours (which also are affected by protease but to a much lesser degree).

In my baking life I have sought out clear tutorials and recipes for making different wild starters. Over the years I've found myself somewhat impatient, largely because so many of the starter instructions were overly elaborate and confusing. I imagine others could relate, and might prefer some straightforward steps, considering that creating a wild starter can feel like a leap of faith for various reasons. Perhaps like me, you have such doubts—or maybe you are concerned if the starter will work at all, or what will happen if you forget to feed it, or you're pondering the price of teff flour and the quantity needed to build the "mother." When taking on an unfamiliar project I prefer to follow a straightforward and direct map, which is what I provide here for all of you new sourdough adventurers. The recipe for building the mother wild starter is very concise, and, I expect you will begin seeing a lot of bubbly action and signs of life after three or four days.

As far as bread is concerned, my true affinity lies with sourdough breads made from scratch with wild starters. Creating yeast from one's very own kitchen, which brings great flavor and nourishment to bread, is incredibly appealing. Sourdough starters imbue a rich complex flavor that is quite scrumptious and very enjoyable. It must be noted that the nurturing and wholesome breads in this chapter are indeed stout and substantial, and certainly not as light as my yeasted breads. Nonetheless, they are equally delicious and in my opinion, even more nutritious. For the lightest of the breads in this chapter, I recommend Potato Rosemary Bread (page 91), Multiple Grain Wild Starter

Boule (page 80), and Buckwheat Boule (page 83). For the diehard quinoa fans and health nuts, the Soft Quinoa Sourdough (page 92) is spectacular and full of quinoa flavor. All of the wild starter breads are full of flavor and will accompany any meal with an earthy and elegant panache!

✦ ✦ ✦ ✦ ✦

Wild Starter Tips and Techniques

It was a wonderful surprise to discover just how smooth and manageable it is to create and maintain a wild starter. In this chapter the first recipe is for creating your culture and what I call the "mother" wild starter. It takes about 48 hours to have a strong culture at the ready for the recipes that follow. Once your culture is active, you will feed the mother about once a week if she is resting in the fridge.

To feed your mother starter, once a week take her out of the fridge and first stir her up. Then discard about half of the wild starter and add 1 cup teff or sorghum flour and 1 cup water. Let her sit in a warm spot for 4 to 6 hours. After she is nice and bubbly, stir well, place the lid back on, and return to the fridge. Once a month I like to transfer my starter to a clean mason jar.

If you find yourself addicted to baking frequently (using your starter every other day or daily), you'll want to feed her every time you bake. Stir her well before removing the ¼ cup for the production levain (in almost every recipe ¼ cup is called for), then discard an additional ¼ cup of starter. Then add ¼ cup teff or sorghum flour and ¼ cup water; stir well, let her sit again for 4 to 6 hours, and return her to the fridge with the lid on.

If you have taken the time to create this starter but are not using her very often, no need to worry! Perhaps you can picture yourself baking wild starter sourdough homemade breads in the next season. That is okay! You can freeze your wild starter. Here's how: Feed her, then give her ample time to become active by letting her warm up for a little over 4 hours. Then pour ¼ cup quantities into ice cube trays and freeze. Transfer the frozen cubes to a sealed container in your freezer. One day prior to baking, remove one frozen cube from the freezer and place in a bowl on the kitchen counter so it has time to thaw before you make your production levain.

You may be wondering, just what is a production levain? In almost every wild starter recipe, ¼ cup of my mother wild starter is mixed with fresh flour and water and set aside for about 4 hours in a warm spot to refresh and become more active with yeast liveliness. Our wild starter is made of many yeasts and does not behave as vigorously as the single-strain yeast used in yeasted bread recipes, and so this step is gentler than a similar step in a yeast bread recipe. We are actually *making* the active yeast rather than pouring it from a package. It is as if we are awakening the sleeping mother wild starter and arousing the yeasts—similar to what happens when commercial yeast is mixed with sweetener and water.

Other than the production levain step, a great deal of the information found in Yeasted Bread Tips and Techniques (page 8) applies to these recipes. It would be beneficial to revisit this section prior to rolling up your sleeves and fastening on an apron. In particular, you might review the shaping and dough-handling guidelines, scoring instructions, and the most advantageous way to combine the ingredients. Be sure to also note the helpful directions about working with a water bath in your oven.

A few more pointers that I will also reiterate in some of the recipes: In creating the initial culture and the mother wild starter, it is very important to remove the apple skin and cabbage leaves after 48 hours. Please be sure to do this so that your mother starter doesn't mold or develop any off-putting flavors! Another tip for this initial culture (as well as when you are developing your production levain), is to cover your mason jar or bowl with a linen cloth should it be fruit fly season. Linen is ideal because its weave is not very tight, providing ample room for the microbes in the air to come down and make a new life in the starter. Otherwise I actually prefer to leave the jar uncovered in a warm spot in my kitchen. On top of the refrigerator is a terrific spot, taking advantage of the heat rinsing from the back.

Lastly, to keep things organized and simple, I propose keeping a calendar in the kitchen for making notes as to when you fed your starter last. Upon first creating the initial culture and feeding it every 12 hours for 48 hours, it is easy to forget what day and feeding you are in. Notes on a calendar can take away that ambiguity. Have trust in this process and yourself. Yeast is alive and everywhere, and you are just about to propagate some in a mason jar with flour and water—enjoy appreciating something that is invisible to us most of the time!

✦ Mother Wild Starter ✦

Creating a wild starter is like a fun home science project. It is quite easy to do and well worth the effort. As your starter becomes a part of your baking life and you are in a feeding rhythm, you may enjoy feeding your starter other high-protein, gluten-free flours such as sorghum flour, garbanzo bean flour, amaranth flour, or quinoa flour. To get started, follow the instructions below; after about 3 days you will be ready to make your first bread with this wild starter. Please do read Wild Starter Tips and Techniques (page 76) for detailed instructions on refreshing and storing your starter.

◇◇◇◇◇◇◇◇◇◇◇◇◇◇◇◇◇◇◇◇◇◇◇ **MAKES ½ OF A GALLON JAR** ◇◇◇◇◇◇◇◇◇◇◇◇◇◇◇◇◇◇◇◇◇◇◇

5 cups (1 pound, 12 ounces) teff flour

5 cups room temperature filtered water

2 purple cabbage leaves

Skin from ½ medium apple (any type)

1. Place 1 cup of the teff flour and 1 cup of the water in a large glass gallon jar. Mix thoroughly with a wooden spoon. Add the cabbage leaves and apple skin. Mix again, coating the leaves and peelings well, and let rest in a warm spot (about 70 degrees F) in your kitchen for 12 hours. If it is fruit fly season, you may want to cover the jar with a linen cloth or another cloth with a large weave.

2. Stir periodically as you come and go from the kitchen. After the first 12 hours, add another 1 cup teff flour and 1 cup water. Mix well.

3. Repeat this process every 12 hours. After 48 hours you will see yeast activity and bubbles in your starter. Once the starter is full of life with lots of bubbly activity and foam, remove the cabbage leaves and apple skin using tongs. Now your starter is ready to use in the recipes that follow. Instructions for refreshing and storing can be found on page 76.

✦ Multiple Grain Wild Starter Boule ✦

This is a handsome bread that displays three beautiful scores, reminiscent of tree branches. The exterior makes for a wonderful, strong, crusty crust. The interior is moist with little holes where air pockets rose in the dough. The flavor is slightly tangy from the starter, and the combination of all the flours with the flax meal is delightfully earthy and addictive.

◇◇◇◇◇◇◇◇◇◇◇◇◇◇◇◇◇◇◇◇◇◇◇ **MAKES 1 MEDIUM LOAF** ◇◇◇◇◇◇◇◇◇◇◇◇◇◇◇◇◇◇◇◇◇◇◇

PRODUCTION LEVAIN

¼ cup Mother Wild Starter (p. 79)

1 cup teff flour

½ cup plus 2 tablespoons room temperature filtered water

DOUGH

1 cup teff flour

½ cup millet flour

½ cup flax meal

¼ cup brown rice flour

¼ cup tapioca flour

1 tablespoon olive oil

1 tablespoon maple syrup

1 teaspoon sea salt

¾ cup room temperature filtered water

1. To make the production levain, combine the wild starter with the teff flour and water in a medium glass bowl. Let rest, uncovered or covered with a linen cloth, for about 4 hours. When the levain shows bubbly, yeasty activity, it is ready to mix with the remaining ingredients.

2. Preheat the oven to 450 degrees F and place a water bath on the bottom rack or the oven floor. Lightly grease a sheet pan or line with parchment paper.

3. To make the dough, in a large mixing bowl, combine the production levain with the teff flour, millet flour, flax meal, brown rice flour, tapioca flour, olive oil, maple syrup, salt, and water. Mix well until a soft dough has formed.

4. Turn out the dough onto a work surface dusted with teff flour and gently form into a round boule shape. Transfer the boule to the prepared pan and score with 3 curved lines stemming from one point, each about ⅛ inch deep. Bake for 10 minutes. Decrease the oven temperature to 425 degrees F and bake for an additional 40 minutes, until golden brown and crusty.

✦ Sourdough Baton ✦

This wholesome baton-shaped bread brings a traditional presence to the table and is ideal for a dinner party—or even a picnic. The mellow tang from the wild starter is complemented by the nutty sweetness the other ingredients bring to the bread. The crust is rustic and the inside chewy!

◇◇◇◇◇◇◇◇◇◇◇◇◇◇◇◇◇◇◇◇◇◇ **MAKES 1 LARGE BATON** ◇◇◇◇◇◇◇◇◇◇◇◇◇◇◇◇◇◇◇◇◇◇

PRODUCTION LEVAIN

¼ cup Mother Wild Starter (p. 79)

1 cup teff flour

1 cup room temperature filtered water

DOUGH

1 cup teff flour

½ cup garbanzo bean flour

½ cup flax meal

¼ cup brown rice flour

¼ cup tapioca flour

1 tablespoon canola oil

1 tablespoon maple syrup

1 teaspoon xanthan gum

1 teaspoon sea salt

½ cup room temperature filtered water

1 tablespoon poppy or sesame seeds, for sprinkling

1. To make the production levain, combine the wild starter with the teff flour and water in a medium glass bowl. Let rest, uncovered or covered with a linen cloth, for about 4 hours. When the levain shows bubbly, yeasty activity, it is ready to mix with the remaining ingredients.

2. Preheat the oven to 450 degrees F and place a water bath on the bottom rack or the oven floor. Generously dust a sheet pan with teff flour.

3. To make the dough, in a large mixing bowl, combine the production levain with the teff flour, garbanzo flour, flax meal, brown rice flour, tapioca flour, canola oil, maple syrup, xanthan gum, salt, and water. Mix well until a soft dough has formed.

4. Turn out the dough onto a work surface dusted with teff flour and gently form into a baton shape. I recommend starting the shaping on the counter, then transferring the dough to the prepared sheet pan and finishing the shaping by gently rolling the dough back and forth to elongate the cylinder-like loaf to the length of the pan. Score the baton with 4 or 5 evenly spaced diagonal lines about ⅛ inch deep. Brush the baton with water and sprinkle with the poppy seeds. Bake for 20 minutes. Decrease the oven temperature to 425 degrees F and bake for an additional 50 minutes, until golden brown and crusty.

✦ Buckwheat Boule ✦

Visually, this bread is very attractive and unique with its shiny coat of flax seeds. The earthiness of the buckwheat isn't overpowering, but rather is balanced with the teff flour. Even though it has a strong flavor, it can be paired with most any food or spread. This is a soft, scrumptious loaf, offering a bit of tasty flax seed in each bite.

◇◇◇◇◇◇◇◇◇◇◇◇◇◇◇◇◇◇◇◇ **MAKES 1 SMALL BOULE** ◇◇◇◇◇◇◇◇◇◇◇◇◇◇◇◇◇◇◇◇

PRODUCTION LEVAIN

¼ cup Mother Wild Starter (p. 79)

1 cup teff flour

1 cup room temperature
   filtered water

DOUGH

1 cup teff flour

¾ cup buckwheat flour

1 cup flax seeds, divided

¼ cup tapioca flour

1 tablespoon canola oil

1 tablespoon maple syrup

1 teaspoon xanthan gum

1 teaspoon sea salt

½ cup room temperature
   filtered water

1. Prepare the production levain by combining the wild starter with the teff flour and water in a medium glass bowl. Let rest, uncovered, or covered with a linen cloth, for about 4 hours. When the levain shows bubbly, yeasty activity, it is ready to mix with the remaining ingredients.

2. Preheat the oven to 450 degrees F and place a water bath on the bottom rack or the oven floor. Lightly grease a sheet pan or line with parchment paper.

3. For the dough, in a large mixing bowl, combine the levain with the teff flour, buckwheat flour, ½ cup of the flax seeds, the tapioca flour, canola oil, maple syrup, xanthan gum, salt, and water. Mix well until a soft dough has formed.

4. Turn out the dough onto a work surface dusted with the remaining ½ cup flax seeds and gently form into a round boule shape, coating the dough with the seeds. Transfer the boule to the prepared pan and score by cutting 4 lines into a diamond shape. Bake for 20 minutes. Decrease the oven temperature to 400 degrees F and bake for an additional 1 hour, until crusty and firm to the touch.

✦ Sourdough House Batard ✦

This wholesome batard-style loaf has a very mellow flavor that will show off the characteristics of whatever you serve it with. It's a lovely all-purpose bread that is attractive in its simple appearance, with one score gently placed down the center of the loaf. Because the bread is so versatile, it is a splendid choice to bring to a dinner party.

〰〰〰〰〰〰〰〰〰〰〰〰 **MAKES 1 MEDIUM BATARD** 〰〰〰〰〰〰〰〰〰〰〰〰

Production Levain
¼ cup Mother Wild Starter (p. 79)

1 cup teff flour

½ cup plus 2 tablespoons room temperature filtered water

Dough
1 cup tapioca flour

¾ cup teff flour

½ cup flax meal

¼ cup millet flour

1 tablespoon olive oil

1 tablespoon maple syrup

1 teaspoon sea salt

½ cup plus 2 tablespoons room temperature filtered water

1. Prepare the production levain by combining the wild starter with the teff flour and water in a medium glass bowl. Let rest, uncovered or covered with a linen cloth, for about 4 hours. When the levain shows bubbly, yeasty activity, it is ready to mix with the remaining ingredients.

2. Preheat the oven to 450 degrees F and place a water bath on the bottom rack or the oven floor. Lightly grease a sheet pan or line with parchment paper.

3. For the dough, in a large mixing bowl, combine the production levain with the tapioca flour, teff flour, flax meal, millet flour, olive oil, maple syrup, salt, and water. Mix well until a soft dough has formed.

4. Turn out the dough onto a work surface dusted with teff flour and gently form into a batard shape. Transfer the batard to the prepared pan and score with one line running the length of the loaf, just off center and about ⅛ inch deep. Bake for 10 minutes. Decrease the oven temperature to 425 degrees F and bake for an additional 55 minutes, until golden brown and crusty.

✦ Teff Baton ✦

This is one of the most wholesome, nutritious, and high-fiber breads I've developed so far. I am particularly enthusiastic about this bread because the only flour used is teff. All the ingredients are simple, and the essence of the teff really shines, with its delicious and unique flavor. Indeed, we enjoy this favorite wild starter bread on a regular basis at home.

◇◇◇◇◇◇◇◇◇◇◇◇◇◇◇◇◇◇◇◇◇◇ **MAKES 1 LARGE BATON** ◇◇◇◇◇◇◇◇◇◇◇◇◇◇◇◇◇◇◇◇◇◇

PRODUCTION LEVAIN

¼ cup Mother Wild Starter (p. 79)

1 cup teff flour

½ cup plus 2 tablespoons room temperature filtered water

DOUGH

2 cups teff flour

¼ cup flax meal

1 tablespoon canola oil

1 tablespoon maple syrup

1 teaspoon sea salt

¾ cup room temperature filtered water

1. Prepare the production levain by combining the wild starter with the teff flour and water in a medium glass bowl. Let rest, uncovered or covered with a linen cloth, for about 4 hours. When the levain shows bubbly, yeasty activity, it is ready to mix with the remaining ingredients.

2. Preheat the oven to 450 degrees F and place a water bath on the bottom rack or the oven floor. Generously dust a sheet pan with teff flour.

3. For the dough, in a large mixing bowl, combine the production levain with the teff flour, flax meal, canola oil, maple syrup, salt, and water. Mix well until a soft dough has formed.

4. Turn out the dough onto a work surface dusted with teff flour and gently form into a baton shape. I recommend starting the shaping on the counter and then

transferring the dough to the prepared sheet pan and finishing shaping by gently rolling the dough back and forth to elongate the cylinder-like loaf to the length of the pan. Score the baton with 4 or 5 evenly spaced diagonal lines about ⅛ inch deep. Bake for 10 minutes. Decrease the oven temperature to 425 degrees F and bake for an additional 40 minutes, until golden brown and crusty.

◆ Pumpkin Sage Loaf ◆

This charming autumn loaf bread is very attractive with its warm pumpkin color contrasting with the soft green of the sage leaves. The loaf is delicious on its own, of course, but also makes quite a fetching contribution when served with a hearty bean soup and a crisp salad.

◇◇◇◇◇◇◇◇◇◇◇◇◇◇◇◇◇◇◇◇◇◇◇◇◇ **MAKES 1 LARGE LOAF** ◇◇◇◇◇◇◇◇◇◇◇◇◇◇◇◇◇◇◇◇◇◇◇◇◇

PRODUCTION LEVAIN

¼ cup Mother Wild Starter (p. 79)

1 cup teff flour

1 cup room temperature filtered water

DOUGH

¼ cup fresh sage leaves, chopped, plus 3 to 5 whole leaves, for decoration

3 tablespoons olive oil, divided

½ cup pumpkin purée (canned or fresh)

1 cup teff flour

½ cup garbanzo bean flour

½ cup tapioca flour

¼ cup arrowroot

1½ tablespoons maple syrup

1 teaspoon sea salt

½ cup room temperature filtered water

1. Prepare the production levain by combining the wild starter with the teff flour and water in a medium glass bowl. Let rest, uncovered or covered with a linen cloth, for 4 to 6 hours. When the levain shows bubbly, yeasty activity, it is ready to mix with the remaining ingredients.

2. Preheat the oven to 350 degrees F and lightly grease and flour an 8-by-4-by-4-inch loaf pan.

3. For the dough, sauté the chopped sage leaves in 1 tablespoon of the olive oil over low heat for 4 minutes, until transparent and slightly crisped. Watch very carefully so that the leaves don't over-brown and become bitter.

4. In a large mixing bowl, combine the production levain with the sautéed sage leaves, remaining 2 tablespoons olive oil, pumpkin, teff flour, garbanzo bean flour, tapioca flour, arrowroot, maple syrup, salt, and water. Mix well until a soft dough has formed.

5. With a spatula, guide the dough into the prepared loaf pan. Smooth the surface of the dough with the spatula and gently press the reserved whole sage leaves decoratively into the dough. Bake the bread for 1 hour and 45 minutes, until golden brown and crusty.

✦ Soft Quinoa Sourdough ✦

A sourdough for quinoa lovers! This beautiful bread has an almost cake-like texture and a covering of flax meal and crisscross scores. The flavor of quinoa is dominant but so tasty with a slightly sweet and nutty quality. The ingredients make for an extremely nurturing bread. For a breakfast on the fly, toast a slice and slather with apricot jam!

◇◇◇◇◇◇◇◇◇◇◇◇◇◇◇◇◇◇◇◇◇◇ **MAKES 1 MEDIUM LOAF** ◇◇◇◇◇◇◇◇◇◇◇◇◇◇◇◇◇◇◇◇◇◇

PRODUCTION LEVAIN

¼ cup Mother Wild Starter (p. 79)

1 cup sorghum flour

¾ cup room temperature filtered water

DOUGH

1 cup quinoa flour

1 cup teff flour

½ cup tapioca flour

¾ cup flax meal, divided

2 tablespoons olive oil

1 tablespoon maple syrup

1½ teaspoons sea salt

¾ cup room temperature filtered water

1. Prepare the production levain by combining the wild starter with the sorghum flour and water in a medium glass bowl. Let rest, uncovered or covered with a linen cloth, for about 4 hours. When the levain shows bubbly, yeasty activity, it is ready to mix with the remaining ingredients.

2. Preheat the oven to 350 degrees F. Lightly grease a sheet pan or line with parchment paper.

3. For the dough, in a large mixing bowl, combine the levain with the quinoa flour, teff flour, tapioca flour, ¼ cup of the flax meal, the olive oil, maple syrup, salt, and water. Mix well until a soft dough has formed.

4. Turn out the dough onto a work surface dusted with the remaining ½ cup flax meal and gently form into a round boule shape, coating the dough (especially the top) with the flax meal. Transfer the boule to the prepared pan and score with a crisscross pattern covering the entire loaf. Bake for 2 hours and 20 minutes, until firm to the touch.

✦ Potato Rosemary Bread ✦

This comfort bread, so soft and rounded with potato flavor, has the delightful aroma of rosemary and a wonderfully airy yet firm composition. The crust is hearty and golden due to the initial high temperature of the oven and the steam bath during the first 30 minutes of baking. This bread is unique (along with the injera) in that the starter is mixed directly with the rest of the bread ingredients. I find this instantly gratifying because the production levain step is skipped. For something out of the ordinary and absolutely delectable, I like to use leftovers to make savory french toast for dinner.

◇◇◇◇◇◇◇◇◇◇◇◇◇◇◇◇◇◇◇◇◇ **MAKES 1 MEDIUM LOAF** ◇◇◇◇◇◇◇◇◇◇◇◇◇◇◇◇◇◇◇◇◇

2 tablespoons chia seeds

½ cup water

1½ cups teff flour

1 cup tapioca flour

½ cup arrowroot

½ cup millet flour

½ cup sorghum flour

¼ cup potato flakes

1 tablespoon chopped fresh rosemary

1 teaspoon sea salt

½ cup Mother Wild Starter (p. 79)

3 tablespoons canola oil

2 tablespoons maple syrup

1 cup room temperature filtered water

1. Soak the chia seeds in the ½ cup water for at least 15 minutes. Preheat the oven to 425 degrees F and place a water bath on the bottom rack or the oven floor. Lightly grease a sheet pan or line with parchment paper.

2. In a large mixing bowl, combine the teff flour, tapioca flour, arrowroot, millet flour, sorghum flour, potato flakes, rosemary, and salt.

3. In a separate large mixing bowl (or the bowl of a stand mixer) combine the chia seeds and their soaking liquid, the starter, canola oil, maple syrup, and room temperature water. Add the dry ingredients and mix until a soft dough forms. You can do this by hand with a strong arm and a sturdy spoon, or with your stand mixer and the paddle attachment pulsed on low speed.

4. On a work surface generously dusted with teff flour, turn out the dough and gently form into a round boule shape. Transfer the boule to the prepared pan and score by cutting 4 lines into a diamond score. Bake for 30 minutes. Decrease the temperature to 350 degrees F and bake for an additional 2 hours, until golden brown and crusty.

✦ Walnut–Wild Rice Bread ✦

This is one of my personal favorites. Just a hint of wild rice flour goes a long way here; its flavor is strong and spectacular. When combined with walnuts, it is a marriage of true bliss. There is very little tapioca flour, but just enough to lend lightness. The other flours all support each other in creating an overall mild and delightful taste while showing off the wild rice flavor.

◇◇◇◇◇◇◇◇◇◇◇◇◇◇◇◇◇◇◇◇ **MAKES 1 MEDIUM LOAF** ◇◇◇◇◇◇◇◇◇◇◇◇◇◇◇◇◇◇◇◇

PRODUCTION LEVAIN

¼ cup Mother Wild Starter (p. 79)

1 cup teff flour

1 cup room temperature
   filtered water

DOUGH

1 cup teff flour

½ cup garbanzo bean flour

½ cup flax meal

½ cup walnuts, finely chopped

¼ cup wild rice flour

¼ cup tapioca flour

1 tablespoon canola oil

1 tablespoon maple syrup

1 teaspoon xanthan gum

1 teaspoon sea salt

½ cup room temperature
   filtered water

1. Prepare the production levain by combining the wild starter with the teff flour and water in a medium glass bowl. Let rest, uncovered or covered with a linen cloth, for about 4 hours. When the levain shows bubbly, yeasty activity, it is ready to mix with the remaining ingredients.

2. Preheat the oven to 450 degrees F and place a water bath on the bottom rack or the oven floor. Lightly grease a sheet pan or line with parchment paper.

3. For the dough, in a large mixing bowl, combine the production levain with the teff flour, garbanzo bean flour, flax meal, walnuts, wild rice flour, tapioca flour, canola oil, maple syrup, xanthan gum, salt, and water. Mix well until a soft dough has formed.

4. Turn out the dough onto a work surface dusted with teff flour and gently form into a round boule shape. Transfer the boule to the prepared pan and score by cutting 4 lines into a diamond score. Bake for 15 minutes. Decrease the oven temperature to 400 degrees F and bake for an additional 1 hour and 15 minutes, until golden brown and crusty.

✦ Pumpkin-Rosemary Bread with Biga ✦

This recipe is unique in this book because it calls for a biga as the starter. A biga is a small amount of dough that ferments prior to being added to other ingredients, creating a fresh dough that has a sourdough flavor without going to the trouble of making a wild starter. This is a nice option for those who would love a bit more of a sourdough taste (as well as less yeast in their bread), but may not have the ambition or desire to create and maintain a wild starter. The biga comes together in 6 to 8 hours. I recommend combining the biga ingredients in the morning, then finishing the dough in the late afternoon. I first made the loaf without xanthan gum and the bread was extremely tasty, with a very crackled top. Aesthetically, however, the bread is prettier with a teaspoon of xanthan gum added to the dough because the crust will come out smoother. Either way you will be sure to enjoy this savory herb bread!

◇◇◇◇◇◇◇◇◇◇◇◇◇◇◇◇◇◇◇◇◇ **MAKES 1 MEDIUM LOAF** ◇◇◇◇◇◇◇◇◇◇◇◇◇◇◇◇◇◇◇◇◇

BIGA

¼ teaspoon active dry yeast

1 cup teff flour

1 cup room temperature filtered water

DOUGH

1 cup teff flour

½ cup garbanzo bean flour

½ cup tapioca flour

½ cup arrowroot

½ cup pumpkin purée (canned or fresh)

2 tablespoons olive oil

1 tablespoon chopped fresh rosemary

1 tablespoon maple syrup

1 teaspoon xanthan gum (optional)

1 teaspoon sea salt

¼ cup room temperature filtered water

1. Prepare the biga by combining the yeast, teff flour, and water in a medium glass bowl. Let rest, uncovered or covered with a linen cloth, for 6 to 8 hours. When the biga shows bubbly, yeasty activity, it is ready to mix with the remaining ingredients.

2. Preheat the oven to 450 degrees F and place a water bath on the bottom rack or the oven floor. Lightly grease a sheet pan or line with parchment paper.

3. For the dough, in a large mixing bowl, combine the biga with the teff flour, garbanzo bean flour, tapioca flour, arrowroot, pumpkin, olive oil, rosemary, maple syrup, xanthan gum, salt, and water. Mix well until a soft dough has formed.

4. Turn out the dough onto a work surface dusted with teff flour and gently form into a round boule shape. Transfer the boule to the prepared sheet pan and score with a semicircle. Bake for 20 minutes. Decrease the oven temperature to 425 degrees F and bake for an additional 1 hour, until crusty and firm to the touch.

FLATBREADS

THE FIRST FLATBREAD **I** MADE was *carta di musica* (a paper-thin Italian flatbread that translates as "sheet of music"). I was wholeheartedly enamored with the process. With flour dusting my entire countertop, little balls of dough waited in a line to be rolled out into thin oblong shapes and then brushed with olive oil and sea salt. While one tray was baking, I would be readying the next and peeking through the oven window to witness little air pockets puffing up and turning the bread a golden brown in some spots and darker in others. Then we would sit down to a meal and pick up a bit of savory this and that off our plates and scoop it up with a bite of flatbread—it was almost too delicious!

Since that first experience, I have paid closer attention to flatbreads, a rich part of so many cultures. Their presence at mealtime has been—and is presently—of great importance all over the world. Some flatbreads are valued for religious sentiment and symbolism, while others serve as a utensil for picking up other scrumptious parts of the meal, as with the Ethiopian injera and the Indian roti. And in other cultures flatbreads are a deep-rooted part of the tradition of cuisine.

Flatbreads were a part of our ancestors' lives before puffier leavened breads and long before breads baked in rectangular loaf pans. One of the predominant influences that shaped what our predecessors ate was the kind of oven available. (Isn't this still the case? How our landscapes and our cultures change with our inventions!) Back in 3000 BC, the first ovens were portable, small, and made of clay. Flour, water, and salt were mixed together, rolled out, and then baked—often on the side of the beehive-shaped clay oven. Later, in the nineteenth century, larger ovens, much like the wood-fired ovens producing artisan breads and pizzas at bread festivals and farmers' markets today, came into use. In Europe, dating as far back as medieval times and before household ovens were common, our ancestors used (what I find to be so rustically handsome) community bakehouses made of stone and brick. The lack of home ovens meant that some of the later flatbread recipes were made on a griddle or stovetop. Oat farls and crumpets are a couple of examples of these stovetop flatbreads.

One of my favorite flatbread recipes is Lilli's Carta di Musica (page 105). My secret to creating great recipes is having my daughter present during the creative process. As a matter of fact, it is a verifiable truth in our household that if I make a new bread without Lilli, it turns out "a little funny." We have an unusually large counter that Lilli sits on while we bake. She recommends a hint of wild rice flour if the dough ought to be a touch firmer, or in the case of flatbreads, how thin she would like them rolled out. Lilli's Carta di Musica was created with much more of Lilli's influence than mine and it is *squisito*!

Some of the age-old flatbread recipes, such as the arepas, oat farls, and injera, actually originated with gluten-free flours, and I have only slightly adapted them to make the recipes vegan, or to add a personal touch. Isn't that something special? Do you feel for a moment a connection to a delicious sustenance that runs deep into our history?

If you have shifted to a gluten-free diet for health reasons, you are likely feeling much better physically—but perhaps you also feel like an outcast from our wheat-centric heritage. Do you miss the ability to enjoy a piece of tart with friends at a neighborhood patisserie, bakery, or boulangerie? Or maybe you feel like you are imposing on friends when invited to dinner and must awkwardly remind the host that you don't eat gluten. In the throes of this lonely feeling, it might seem that you are the first person not to share a croissant, baguette, slice of rye bread, paratha, or mantou, and that all "real" breads have always been made with wheat. And yet, here we have three venerable flatbread recipes—Arepas (page 112), Oat Farls (page 115), and Injera (page 121)—that are already gluten-free and practically unaltered from the age-old recipes. And there are so many more! Do spend some time on the Internet and find potato farls, dosas, corn tortillas, and more! If you have felt somewhat desolate in your shift to gluten-free, I hope you can start to engage in a new perspective celebrating this connection to some of our oldest—gluten-free—flatbreads.

Here you will find flatbread recipes inspired from around the world. Some are yeast-free, a few are made with my wild starter, and some are made with single-strain yeast. All are scrumptious! The variety of flavors from one to the next is surprising and exciting in the most mouthwatering way!

✦ ✦ ✦ ✦ ✦

FLATBREAD TIPS AND TECHNIQUES

Making flatbreads builds baking confidence! The handling of the doughs doesn't require much finesse, as they are very sturdy and forgiving. They are different from all of the other doughs in this book because you don't need to worry about using too much flour in the shaping process. If you are making flatbread with a youngster who is enjoying a little mountain of flour and reworking the dough, it will still turn out scrumptious. I usually give Lilli her own piece of dough to roll and flatten while I work on the remaining dough. Naturally, flatbreads may be somewhat laborious, as they demand a bit of repetitiveness in rolling out and flattening. But on the other hand, all that rolling can be great fun!

In the recipes that follow I suggest a certain thickness for each particular flatbread. In many cases a rolling pin will work best to work the dough, but in other cases the palm of your hand works better. In each recipe I suggest one or the other. When shaping by hand, it's best to start by lining your sheet pan with parchment paper and dusting the paper with a fine coating of brown rice flour. You can dust your sheet pan very liberally with brown rice flour instead of using parchment, but I recommend using parchment (now available at most grocery stores) because it is so satisfying to have the delicious baked flatbread pop easily off the paper with very little mess. More often than not, I shake off any residue from the used parchment paper and save it to use again.

Most recipes call for 8 portions. Roll the balls in brown rice flour or teff flour so that they have a fine coating of flour to prevent sticking. Keep your hands clean, and dry, and dusted with flour; you may find yourself washing your hands once or twice before all the balls are flattened. If using your hands to make the thicker flatbreads, press down on a ball of dough with your palm, still on the counter, and shape it into a circle or oval about ¾ inch thick. Then transfer the dough to the sheet pan and press it to its suggested thickness. These are strong doughs, but since they are pressed to a minimal thickness, and because they don't stretch like a wheat dough does, the final pressing directly on the sheet pan prevents tearing after flattening.

For the recipes that call for rolling out the dough, here is another unusual and very helpful trick: Tear off a sheet of parchment paper to fit the length of your sheet pan. Instead of placing the paper on the pan, put it on your work surface (most likely your kitchen counter). Dust the paper generously, place your tennis ball of dough on the paper, and press slightly with your floured hand. Now sprinkle more flour on top and roll out the ball with your rolling pin to a not-quite-paper-thin, beautifully amorphous shape. If the dough tears, use your hand to gently press the tear back together. But keep in mind that it is natural and attractive to have a few small tears around the perimeter. Now, with scissors, cut the parchment paper around the paper-thin flatbread and slide the dough and paper right onto your sheet pan. Repeat with the rest of the dough. When all the dough has been rolled and placed on a sheet pan, you are ready to top with olive oil, sea salt, and sesame seeds or bake as is. I like to bake some flatbreads without a brushing of oil, as their surface is so soft and floury when popped right into the oven naked. Then of course you have the option to dip the finished flatbread in olive oil or other flavored oils.

Not all of the flatbread recipes in this chapter are flattened with pressing and rolling. Some, like the injera, arepas, and oat farls, are cooked in a skillet. The flatbread recipes that we handle in a different fashion are not very finicky, and the techniques described are easy to follow. The focaccia doughs are very pliable and easily relax into an oval or rounded rectangle with some gentle encouragement by your baking hands.

Lastly, two of the flatbread recipes require the wild starter: the Injera (page 121) and the Flatbreads for Nonni (page 107). Please review the ingredients of each recipe before jumping in to be sure you are prepared—if you haven't made the wild starter yet, you will want to allow 48 hours to do so.

You are now ready to plunge into the beautiful and harmonious mess of flatbread making!

✦ Lilli's Carta di Musica ✦

This recipe, high up on my list of favorites, is very much a creation of my daughter Lilli. She suggested the touch of wild rice flour, as well as the inclusion of garbanzo bean flour. She also insisted on a paper-thin flatbread because, I believe, she so enjoyed rolling out each piece of dough. The thinner the flatbread, the longer one must spend rolling it out, you see. Well, the result was really spectacular! The flatbreads are delicious when brushed with olive oil and then sprinkled with sea salt before baking. You might try leaving some sans olive oil and some with to see which way you like best! Either way, enjoy with olives and fresh figs. Or make a bruschetta topping and scoop up the bright Italian flavors with this beautiful flatbread.

◇◇◇◇◇◇◇◇◇◇◇◇◇◇◇◇◇◇◇◇◇ **MAKES 8 FLATBREADS** ◇◇◇◇◇◇◇◇◇◇◇◇◇◇◇◇◇◇◇◇◇

2 tablespoons chia seeds

½ cup water

1 cup teff flour

½ cup garbanzo bean flour

½ cup sorghum flour

¼ cup arrowroot

¼ cup tapioca flour

1 tablespoon wild rice flour

1 teaspoon sea salt

2 teaspoons active dry yeast

¾ cup room temperature
   filtered water

2 tablespoons canola oil

1 tablespoon maple syrup

Coarse sea salt, for sprinkling

1. Soak the chia seeds in the ½ cup water for at least 15 minutes. Preheat the oven to 425 degrees F.

2. In a large mixing bowl, combine the teff flour, garbanzo bean flour, sorghum flour, arrowroot, tapioca flour, wild rice flour, and salt.

3. In a separate large mixing bowl (or the bowl of a stand mixer), dissolve the yeast in the room temperature water. Add the canola oil and maple syrup. Just as the yeast begins to foam and feed on the maple syrup, about 3 minutes, add the combined dry ingredients and the chia seeds with their soaking liquid. Mix just until a soft dough forms. You can do this by hand with a strong arm and a

sturdy spoon, or with your stand mixer and the paddle attachment pulsed on low speed.

4. Divide the dough into 8 balls about the size of a tennis ball. Roll each ball in brown rice flour or teff flour so that it has a fine coating to prevent sticking. Tear off a sheet of parchment paper the length of your sheet pan and place on your work surface. Dust the paper generously with brown rice flour or teff flour, place one ball of dough on the paper, and press slightly with your floured clean hand to about a ½-inch thickness. Sprinkle more flour on top and roll out the dough with a rolling pin to a thickness that is not quite paper thin, with a beautifully amorphous shape. Mend any tear by gently pressing it back together. With scissors, cut the parchment paper around the dough and slide the paper and dough onto a sheet pan. Repeat with the rest of the dough.

5. Sprinkle the flatbreads with coarse sea salt and bake for 15 minutes, until golden brown. Check on them while baking especially if they are brushed with olive oil. If your oven bakes unevenly, you may need to pull out one tray of flatbreads early or rearrange the trays halfway through the baking process for more even baking.

✦ Flatbreads for Nonni ✦

One recent sunny spring afternoon, Lilli's grandmother, Nonni Kat, came to share a leisurely lunch with us outside. I had wanted to make her some special bread to take home and enjoy with Boppa (Lilli's grandfather), but I was surprised to find my cupboards a bit bare—and that I was out of some of the flours I had intended to use to create her special loaf. I know she loves flatbreads, and what ensued was the following recipe. It was a spectacular success! I believe the potato flour is key to the delicious, favorable outcome. These flatbreads are full of flavor but not overpowering, soft, and very satisfying. Please note this recipe calls for using some wild starter.

◇◇◇◇◇◇◇◇◇◇◇◇◇◇◇◇◇◇◇◇ MAKES 4 FLATBREADS ◇◇◇◇◇◇◇◇◇◇◇◇◇◇◇◇◇◇◇◇

2 tablespoons chia seeds	1 tablespoon tapioca flour
½ cup water	1 teaspoon sea salt
1 cup quinoa flour	1 tablespoon olive oil
½ cup arrowroot	1 tablespoon maple syrup
¼ cup flax meal	1 cup Mother Wild Starter (p. 79)
2 tablespoons potato flour	

1. Soak the chia seeds in the water for at least 15 minutes. Preheat the oven to 425 degrees F. Line 2 sheet pans with parchment paper and lightly dust with brown rice flour.

2. In a large mixing bowl, combine the quinoa flour, arrowroot, flax meal, potato flour, tapioca flour, and salt.

3. In a separate large mixing bowl (or the bowl of a stand mixer), combine the chia seeds and their soaking liquid with the olive oil, maple syrup, and wild starter. Add the combined dry ingredients and mix until the dough is soft and holding together. This will happen sooner than you may expect. If you are using a stand mixer, insert the paddle attachment and pulse on low speed. Otherwise, a wooden spoon will certainly do the trick.

4. Turn the dough out onto a work surface generously dusted with brown rice flour and divide into 4 portions. Gently place 2 portions of dough on each sheet pan and using your clean, dry and floured hands, press into oblong shapes between ⅛ inch and ¼ inch thick. With the edge of your hand, make 3 ridges lengthwise on the surface of each loaf. Bake for 25 minutes, until golden and firm to the touch. Serve warm. Or later, reheat the breads by wrapping in aluminum foil and placing in a hot oven for 5 to 10 minutes.

✦ Matzo ✦

This recipe was created for my holiday cookbook, but it is an excellent flatbread recipe to include here, as it is used to create so many other wonderful foods, such as matzo balls and fancy desserts. All of my other flatbreads are intended for eating as they are, but this one is designed to be a gluten-free vegan matzo to use in other recipes that call for matzo.

〰〰〰〰〰〰〰〰〰〰〰〰〰〰〰 **MAKES 1 MATZO** 〰〰〰〰〰〰〰〰〰〰〰〰〰〰〰

1 cup brown rice flour

½ cup coconut flour

1½ cups room temperature filtered water

1. Preheat the oven to 350 degrees F. Line sheet pan with parchment paper and lightly dust with brown rice flour. In the bowl of a stand mixer or a bowl with a mixing spoon, combine the brown rice flour, coconut flour, and water and mix until a smooth dough forms.

2. Press the dough out onto a sheet pan, forming a 10-inch circle. Using a fork, prick the dough with holes. Bake for 40 minutes, until crackly and firm to the touch.

✦ Quinoa Salt-and-Pepper Crackers ✦

This is a delightful recipe I developed for my second cookbook, Gluten-Free and Vegan Holidays. I felt it had to be included here for those who do not have that cookbook. These are sophisticated and welcoming crackers that make a fine introduction to a dinner gathering.

◇◇◇◇◇◇◇◇◇◇◇◇◇◇◇◇◇ **MAKES ABOUT 1 DOZEN CRACKERS** ◇◇◇◇◇◇◇◇◇◇◇◇◇◇◇◇◇

1½ cups quinoa flour

¼ cup coconut oil

1 teaspoon baking soda

½ teaspoon sea salt, plus additional for sprinkling

Freshly ground black pepper

½ cup room temperature filtered water

1. Preheat the oven to 350 degrees F. Lightly dust a sheet pan with quinoa flour.

2. In the bowl of a stand mixer fitted with the paddle attachment, mix the quinoa flour, coconut oil, baking soda, salt, pepper, and water on low speed.

3. Press the dough into a 12-inch tart pan, prick all over with a fork, and sprinkle with additional salt and pepper. Alternatively, roll out the dough on a work surface dusted with quinoa flour to about ⅛ inch thick. Cut out shapes. With a spatula, transfer the shapes to the sheet pan, prick with a fork, and sprinkle with more freshly ground pepper and sea salt.

4. Bake the crackers in the tart pan or on the sheet pan for 20 minutes, until crisp and golden. If using the tart pan, as soon as the cracker comes out of oven, score into wedges. Let the crackers cool for 1 hour before transferring to a plate or a cookie tin to store.

✦ Arepas ✦

These Venezuelan corn cakes are crisp on the outside with wonderfully soft middles. They are sensational served with spicy salsa, or a mild almond cheese or soft spread. In Venezuela they are often used as one would use a sandwich bread or roll, by slicing them open and stuffing with sautéed onions and peppers.

◇◇◇◇◇◇◇◇◇◇◇◇◇◇◇◇◇◇◇◇◇◇◇ **MAKES 6 TO 8 AREPAS** ◇◇◇◇◇◇◇◇◇◇◇◇◇◇◇◇◇◇◇◇◇◇◇

1 cup cooked polenta or precooked cornmeal

¼ teaspoon salt

1¼ cups boiling water

1½ tablespoons canola oil

1. Preheat the oven to 400 degrees F. Generously grease a sheet pan.

2. In a large bowl, mix together the polenta and salt. Pour in the boiling water and mix with a wooden spoon to form a dough. Cover with a towel and let it rest for 5 to 10 minutes.

3. Using wet hands, form 6 to 8 balls of dough, using about ⅓ cup of dough for each. Press each to form a ¾-inch-thick cake about 2½ inches in diameter. If the dough cracks at the edges, mix in a little more water and then form again.

4. Heat the canola oil in a sauté pan or skillet over medium-high heat. Sauté the cakes until they have a golden crust, about 6 minutes each side.

5. Transfer the cakes to the prepared baking sheet and bake for 15 to 20 minutes, until golden and firm to the touch. Serve hot out of the oven!

⟡ Sardinian Flatbreads ⟡

Rosemary makes her presence known in this slightly crisp flatbread. A little softer than a cracker, yet more delicate and crusty, this traditional southern Italian recipe is so tasty! I prefer mine to be just a touch pliable, but if you would like a crisper flatbread, increase the baking time by 7 to 10 minutes. These are also delicious brushed with olive oil and then sprinkled with sea salt before baking. You might try leaving some sans olive oil and some with to see which you like the best!

⬦⬦⬦⬦⬦⬦⬦⬦⬦⬦⬦⬦⬦⬦⬦⬦⬦⬦⬦⬦ **MAKES 8 FLATBREADS** ⬦⬦⬦⬦⬦⬦⬦⬦⬦⬦⬦⬦⬦⬦⬦⬦⬦⬦⬦⬦

1½ cups teff flour

½ cup garbanzo bean flour

½ cup tapioca flour

½ cup flax meal

1 teaspoon dried rosemary

1 teaspoon sea salt

¾ teaspoon xanthan gum

2 teaspoons active dry yeast

1¼ cups room temperature filtered water

2 tablespoons extra-virgin olive oil

1 tablespoon maple syrup

Coarse sea salt, for sprinkling

1. Preheat the oven to 350 degrees F.

2. In a large mixing bowl, combine the teff flour, garbanzo bean flour, tapioca flour, flax meal, rosemary, salt, and xanthan gum.

3. In a separate large mixing bowl (or the bowl of a stand mixer), dissolve the yeast in the room temperature water. Add the olive oil and maple syrup. Just as the yeast begins to foam and feed on the maple syrup, about 3 minutes, add the combined dry ingredients. Mix well to the point where you have a lovely, pliable bread dough. Because my bread doughs are wetter than traditional bread doughs, you may be surprised at how quickly the dough comes together. Mix thoroughly until the dough holds together, at which point please do not continue mixing the dough. Go ahead and use your stand mixer with a paddle pulsed on low speed, or if you prefer to use your arm and a wooden spoon,

by all means enjoy this slightly slower but very effective way of mixing your bread dough!

4. Divide the dough into 8 balls about the size of a tennis ball. Roll each ball in brown rice flour or teff flour so that it has a fine coating of flour to prevent sticking. Tear off a sheet of parchment paper the length of your sheet pan and place on your work surface. Dust the paper generously with brown rice flour or teff flour, place one ball of dough on the paper, and press it slightly with your floured clean hand to about a ½-inch thickness. Sprinkle more flour on top and roll out with a rolling pin to a thickness that is not quite paper thin, with a beautifully amorphous shape. Mend any tear by gently pressing it back together. With scissors, cut the parchment paper around the dough and slide the paper and dough onto a sheet pan. Repeat with the rest of the dough.

5. Sprinkle the flatbreads with coarse sea salt and bake for 25 minutes, until golden and firm to the touch.

◆ Oat Farls ◆

This old-world Irish recipe originally called for bacon fat. I have replaced the bacon fat with canola oil and the substitution works beautifully. Coconut oil is also a very tasty option but you will notice the coconut flavor coming through, which may or may not be desirable. These oat cakes are fantastic for breakfast with hot tea and marmalade. Actually the apricot filling recipe on page 57 makes for an ambrosial topping of thick jam that isn't overly sweet. Extra oat farls will keep well in a tin for three days, but they are tastiest hot off the griddle.

<><><><><><><><><><><><><><><> **MAKES 16 OAT FARLS** <><><><><><><><><><><><><><><>

2 cups cooked gluten-free oatmeal

⅛ teaspoon baking soda

⅛ teaspoon salt

1 tablespoon plus 1 teaspoon
   canola oil

1½ tablespoons hot water

Gluten-free rolled oats,
   for kneading

Coconut oil or canola oil,
   for the pan

1. Combine the oatmeal, baking soda, and salt in a large bowl. Add the canola oil and hot water, stirring constantly to make a stiff paste. Working rather quickly so as to form the rounds while the dough is still warm, divide the dough into 4 equal portions. Roll each portion into a ball and knead with hands covered in oatmeal to prevent sticking. Knead just until soft and pliable.

2. With a rolling pin and extra oats, roll out one ball to a ¼-inch thickness. Using a 9-inch plate as a template, cut out a round. Repeat with the remaining dough balls. Cut each rolled-out circle into quarters.

3. Heat a griddle or large frying pan over medium heat and lightly grease with canola oil or coconut oil. Place a few wedges as will fit in the pan or griddle and cook for just under 4 minutes, until the edges curl slightly. Turn and cook the other sides for 4 minutes, until crisp and firm. Repeat with the remaining wedges until all the oat cakes are cooked through.

✦ Iranian Barbari Flatbreads ✦

Iranian Barbari bread is often enjoyed for breakfast. I find this flatbread to be a welcome, nourishing accompaniment to any meal though! It is crusty on the outside, yet retains a soft interior, and the sesame seeds on top add great texture.

◇◇◇◇◇◇◇◇◇◇◇◇◇◇◇◇◇◇ **MAKES 2 MEDIUM FLATBREADS** ◇◇◇◇◇◇◇◇◇◇◇◇◇◇◇◇◇◇

1 tablespoon chia seeds

¼ cup water

½ cup brown rice flour

½ cup tapioca flour

¼ cup garbanzo bean flour

¼ cup sorghum flour

¼ cup almond meal

1 teaspoon sea salt

1 teaspoon active dry yeast

½ cup room temperature filtered water

1 tablespoon canola oil, plus additional for brushing

1½ teaspoons Sucanat

1 tablespoon sesame seeds

1. Soak the chia seeds in the ¼ cup water for at least 15 minutes. Preheat the oven to 350 degrees F. Line 2 sheet pans with parchment paper and lightly dust with brown rice flour.

2. In a large mixing bowl, combine the brown rice flour, tapioca flour, garbanzo bean flour, sorghum flour, almond meal, and salt.

3. In a separate large mixing bowl (or the bowl of a stand mixer), dissolve the yeast in the room temperature water. Add the canola oil and Sucanat. Just as the yeast begins to foam and feed on the Sucanat, about 3 minutes, add the combined dry ingredients and the chia seeds with their soaking liquid. Mix thoroughly but just until the dough holds together. This will take just a few moments. You can do this by hand with a strong arm and a sturdy spoon, or with your stand mixer and the paddle attachment pulsed on low speed.

4. Turn the dough out onto a work surface that has been generously dusted with brown rice flour. Divide into 2 portions. Gently place 1 portion on each sheet

pan and using your clean, dry, and floured hands, press into oblong loaves with a scant ¼-inch thickness. With the edge of your hand, make 3 ridges lengthwise on the surface of the dough. Brush the formed doughs with canola oil and sprinkle the sesame seeds on top. Bake for 25 minutes, until golden and firm. Serve warm. Or later, reheat the breads by wrapping them in aluminum foil and placing in a hot oven for 5 to 10 minutes.

✦ Indian Roti ✦

Warm roti is so soft and deliciously mild tasting, ready to wrap up around stronger curries and chutneys. It can be wrapped in aluminum foil and reheated in the oven if you find yourself with leftovers. The flatbread is made with a cast iron skillet or griddle; if you do not have either, a large frying pan will work. One of my friends has actually served these rotis as tortillas and loved it. So even though my intention was to create an Indian roti, please use your imagination to enjoy this versatile flatbread with many cuisines.

◇◇◇◇◇◇◇◇◇◇◇◇◇◇◇◇◇◇◇◇◇◇◇ **MAKES 8 ROTIS** ◇◇◇◇◇◇◇◇◇◇◇◇◇◇◇◇◇◇◇◇◇◇◇

1 tablespoon chia seeds

½ cup water

½ cup brown rice flour

½ cup garbanzo bean flour

½ cup millet flour

½ cup sorghum flour

½ cup tapioca flour

½ cup flax meal

1 teaspoon sea salt

2 tablespoons extra-virgin olive oil

1 tablespoon maple syrup

¾ cup room temperature filtered water

1. Soak the chia seeds in the ½ cup water for at least 15 minutes.

2. In a large mixing bowl, combine the brown rice flour, garbanzo bean flour, millet flour, sorghum flour, tapioca flour, flax meal, and salt.

3. In a separate large mixing bowl (or the bowl of a stand mixer), combine the olive oil, maple syrup, room temperature water, and the chia seeds with their soaking liquid. Add the dry ingredients and mix until a soft dough forms. This will not take long. A stand mixer with a paddle attachment works well, but so will an old-fashioned wooden spoon and a tireless arm.

4. Divide the dough into 8 balls about the size of a tennis ball. Roll the balls in brown rice flour or teff flour so that they have a fine coating to prevent sticking. Be sure to have ample flour on your counter; place one ball on the surface and

press slightly with a floured hand to about a ½-inch thickness. Sprinkle more flour on top of the dough and roll out with a rolling pin until about ⅛ inch thick. Mend any tear by gently pressing it back together.

5. Heat an ungreased griddle over medium heat. Place a roti on the hot griddle and cook on each side for 4 minutes, until golden and firm to the touch. Keep the rotis warm, wrapped in a clean kitchen towel or napkin, while cooking the remaining dough.

✦ Injera ✦

This wonderful Ethiopian flatbread is traditionally used both as a plate and as a kind of utensil, if you will. What a brilliant way to enjoy a meal! The soft bread, full of gorgeous air bubbles, soaks up the surrounding flavors of the meal, which often includes a variety of cooked vegetables, spicy lentils, and beans. The bread is traditionally made solely with teff flour, a wild starter, and a little salt. But at many Ethiopian restaurants in the states, wheat flour is added to the batter.

This recipe is only partly my creation, as it was greatly inspired from a recipe in Peter Reinhart's Whole Grain Breads. I've altered his recipe by adding more water to make the batter a touch thinner. I also leave out the extra yeast because I find that my starter (made with teff flour, cabbage leaves, and water) is quite active. However, if your starter is looking less active, go ahead and add ¼ teaspoon of active dry yeast to the batter. Lastly, I call for a little more salt. Before diving into this recipe, bear in mind that you will need at least 48 hours to create your starter (if she has not yet been created) and an additional 5 hours for the injera dough to ferment. If you plan to have this bread for dinner, make the batter early in the afternoon.

XXXXXXXXXXXXXXXXXXXXXXXXXXXXXXX **MAKES 4 INJERA** XXXXXXXXXXXXXXXXXXXXXXXXXXXXXXX

¼ cup Mother Wild Starter (p. 79)	2 cups room temperature filtered water
1¾ cups teff flour	½ teaspoon salt

1. In a large glass or stainless steel bowl, combine thoroughly the wild starter, teff flour, and water. Let rest for 5 hours, uncovered or covered with a linen cloth.

2. Mix the salt into the batter. Heat a 10-inch skillet or cast iron skillet over medium heat. Wipe the skillet with a paper towel that has been dipped in canola oil. Ladle about 1 cup of batter into the hot skillet, moving and tilting the pan to spread out the batter, almost like you would a crepe. Cook

for about 5 minutes, until the top is cooked through and full of air bubbles. With injera, only one side touches the skillet, so there is no need for flipping! Transfer the injera to a warm plate lined with a cloth and wrap in the cloth to keep it warm. Repeat with the rest of the batter.

✦ Focaccia Simple ✦

This luscious and savory focaccia is chewier and moister than the other focaccia recipes in this cookbook because of the protein-rich garbanzo bean flour. If you are lucky enough to have any leftovers, the thick slices make delectable sandwiches! Imagine a focaccia sandwich of grilled eggplant, fresh tomato, basil, and avocado drizzled with a touch of olive oil and balsamic! Mamma Mia!

◇◇◇◇◇◇◇◇◇◇◇◇◇◇◇◇◇◇◇◇ **MAKES 1 LARGE FOCACCIA** ◇◇◇◇◇◇◇◇◇◇◇◇◇◇◇◇◇◇◇◇

2 tablespoons chia seeds

½ cup water

1 cup teff flour

1 cup tapioca flour

½ cup arrowroot

½ cup sorghum flour

¼ cup garbanzo bean flour

¼ cup millet flour

¼ cup flax meal

2 teaspoons herbes de Provence

1 teaspoon sea salt

1 envelope (2¾ teaspoons) active dry yeast

1 cup room temperature filtered water

5 tablespoons extra-virgin olive oil, divided

2 tablespoons maple syrup

1 large onion, halved and sliced

1. Soak the chia seeds in the ½ cup water for at least 15 minutes. Preheat the oven to 425 degrees F and place a water bath on the bottom rack or the oven floor. Line a sheet pan with parchment paper or grease well and dust with teff or brown rice flour.

2. In a large mixing bowl, combine the teff flour, tapioca flour, arrowroot, sorghum flour, garbanzo bean flour, millet flour, flax meal, herbes de Provence, and salt.

3. In a separate large mixing bowl (or the bowl of a stand mixer), dissolve the yeast in the room temperature water. Add 3 tablespoons of the olive oil and the maple syrup. Just as the yeast begins to foam and feed on the maple syrup, about 3 minutes, add the combined dry ingredients and the chia seeds with

their soaking liquid. Mix well, just until the dough is soft and holding together. This will happen sooner than you may expect. You can do this by hand with a strong arm and a sturdy spoon, or with your stand mixer and the paddle attachment pulsed on low speed.

4. Turn out the dough directly onto the prepared sheet pan. This is a very wet dough and requires little energy to shape. Gently press the dough into an oval that is about ¾ inch thick. Bake on the middle rack for 25 minutes.

5. While the focaccia is baking, sauté the onion. Heat the remaining 2 tablespoons olive oil in a medium skillet over low heat. Add the onion and sauté until it is transparent and just beginning to brown, about 8 minutes.

6. Remove the focaccia from the oven and cover with the sautéed onion. Return the focaccia to the middle rack and bake for an additional 25 minutes, until golden and firm to the touch with a crusty perimeter.

◆ Focaccia *con Gusto* ◆

This focaccia has a most pleasing texture and toppings that are packed with aroma and gusto! I enjoy serving it with a fresh green salad and white bean soup. As the Sicilians say, Mancia di sanu e vivi di malatu! *"Eat with gusto, but drink in moderation!"*

◇◇◇◇◇◇◇◇◇◇◇◇◇◇◇◇◇◇◇◇◇◇ **MAKES 1 LARGE FOCACCIA** ◇◇◇◇◇◇◇◇◇◇◇◇◇◇◇◇◇◇◇◇◇◇

2 tablespoons chia seeds

½ cup water

1 cup teff flour

1 cup sorghum flour

1 cup tapioca flour

¼ cup flax meal

1 teaspoon sea salt

1 envelope (2¾ teaspoons) active dry yeast

1 cup room temperature filtered water

5 tablespoons extra-virgin olive oil, divided

2 tablespoons maple syrup

1 onion, halved and sliced

1 cup reconstituted sun-dried tomatoes, whole

½ cup kalamata olives, whole

1. Soak the chia seeds in the ½ cup water for at least 15 minutes. Preheat the oven to 425 degrees F and place a water bath on the bottom rack or the oven floor. Line a sheet pan with parchment paper or grease well and dust with teff or brown rice flour.

2. In a large mixing bowl, combine the teff flour, sorghum flour, tapioca flour, flax meal, and sea salt.

3. In a separate large mixing bowl (or the bowl of a stand mixer), dissolve the yeast in the room temperature water. Add 3 tablespoons of the olive oil and the maple syrup. Just as the yeast begins to foam and feed on the maple syrup, about 3 minutes, add the combined dry ingredients and the chia seeds with their soaking liquid. Mix just until a soft dough forms. You can do this by hand with a strong arm and a sturdy spoon, or with your stand mixer and the paddle attachment pulsed on low speed.

4. Turn out the dough directly onto the prepared sheet pan. This is a wet dough and requires little energy to shape. Gently press the dough into an oval that is about ¾ inch thick. Bake on the middle rack for 25 minutes.

5. While the focaccia is baking, sauté the onion: Heat the remaining 2 tablespoons olive oil in a medium skillet over low heat. Add the onion and sauté until it is transparent and just beginning to brown, about 8 minutes.

6. Remove the focaccia from the oven and cover with the sautéed onion, sun-dried tomatoes, and olives. Return the focaccia to the middle rack and bake for an additional 25 minutes, until golden and firm to the touch.

✦ Focaccia *con Funghi* ✦

This bread is remarkably tasty and the topping is subtly sweet due to the hint of pinot gris. The development of the recipe preceded that of the Kalamata Olive Bread (page 14). As you may notice, the doughs are very similar! The consistency of this dough was so light yet chewy, I knew it would lend itself well to a bread topped with succulent chantarelle mushrooms.

MAKES 1 LARGE FOCACCIA

TOPPING

3 tablespoons olive oil

1 onion, halved and sliced

2½ cups chopped chanterelle mushrooms

1 teaspoon herbes de Provence

¾ teaspoon sea salt

1 tablespoon pinot gris or other white wine

DOUGH

1 tablespoon chia seeds

½ cup water

1 cup brown rice flour

1 cup tapioca flour

½ cup garbanzo bean flour

½ cup millet flour

½ cup almond meal

⅓ cup flax meal

1 teaspoon sea salt

1 teaspoon xanthan gum

1 envelope (2¾ teaspoons) active dry yeast

1½ cups room temperature filtered water

3 tablespoons canola oil

2 tablespoons Sucanat

1. To make the topping, heat the olive oil in a medium skillet over low heat. Add the onion and sauté until it just begins to brown, about 15 minutes. Add the mushrooms, herbes de Provence, and salt and sauté for an additional 15 minutes. Add the white wine and continue sautéing for a final 8 minutes.

2. To make the dough, soak the chia seeds in the ½ cup water for at least 15 minutes. Preheat the oven to 425 degrees F and place a water bath on the bottom rack or the oven floor. Line a sheet pan with parchment paper or grease well and dust with brown rice flour or teff flour.

3. In a large mixing bowl, combine the brown rice flour, tapioca flour, garbanzo bean flour, millet flour, almond meal, flax meal, salt, and xanthan gum.

4. In a separate large mixing bowl (or the bowl of a stand mixer), dissolve the yeast in the room temperature water. Add the canola oil and Sucanat. Just as the yeast begins to foam and feed on the Sucanat, about 3 minutes, add the combined dry ingredients and the chia seeds with their soaking liquid. Combine well to the point where you have a lovely, pliable bread dough. Because my bread doughs are wetter than traditional bread doughs you may be surprised at how quickly the dough comes together. Go ahead and use your stand mixer with a paddle set on low speed, or if you prefer to use your arm and a wooden spoon, by all means enjoy this slightly slower but very effective way of mixing your bread dough!

5. Turn out the dough directly onto the prepared sheet pan. This is a very wet dough and requires little energy to shape. Gently press into an oval that is about ¾ inch thick. Place on the middle rack of the oven and bake for 25 minutes.

6. Remove the focaccia from the oven. Spread the topping evenly over the top. Return the focaccia to the middle rack and bake for an additional 25 minutes, until golden and firm to the touch with a crusty perimeter.

BATTER BREADS

've included this chapter because I find batter breads to be extremely nourishing and easy to make. The recipes, inspired by Paul Pitchford's beautiful book, *Healing with Whole Foods*, are exceptional in that they require no added yeast or rising agent. You simply mix the flours, grains, and water together and let the batter sit overnight to gain and develop a bit of natural yeast from the surrounding environment. The next day the batter is baked in a loaf pan—and voilà, your nutritious bread is ready!

Batter breads are dense and hearty breads full of rich flavor, and remind me both in weight and texture of a 100 percent rye bread. These in particular have a harder crust with a soft inside. I love the chewy crusts, especially with a little extra salt sprinkled on top. These batter breads are truly delicious.

◆ ◆ ◆ ◆ ◆

BATTER BREAD TIPS AND TECHNIQUES

There really isn't too much to making this style of nourishing bread. You simply combine all the ingredients well in a bowl, then let the batter sit overnight, uncovered, in a warm part of your kitchen. If it is fruit fly season, I suggest covering the bowl with a cloth that has a large weave, such as linen, so the microbes in the surrounding air will still be able to get to the batter. The next day, pour the batter into a loaf pan and top with seeds and sea salt. Then into the oven goes your batter bread to bake, and it is truly as easy as that! To check for doneness, insert a toothpick into the center of the loaf; when it comes out clean, your bread is ready.

Batter breads' hearty crusts (which I go crazy over) demand a different approach to slicing. After the bread has cooled, as unorthodox as this sounds, use a very sharp medium chopping knife, and with a little pressure gently saw through the crust for even, clean slices. Take your time breaking through the crust and then proceed more naturally in cutting through the interior of the bread.

You may feel inspired to substitute different nuts and seeds. Hemp seeds offer a unique flavor and an abundance of nutrition. Other variations might include toasted pecans or finely ground almonds.

These robust and unique batter breads are very satisfying. They offer so much sustenance that I like to serve them alongside light soups and salads. I hope you and yours enjoy these wholesome and hearty breads as much as my family does!

✦ Buckwheat Batter Bread ✦

How this wholesome bread keeps me coming back for more and more! I thoroughly enjoy the overall flavor and experience of the balanced, robust, and tasty loaf. The flours, while equally strong in character, interact in a way that seems lovingly diplomatic: I can taste the flavor of each grain, and even the buckwheat doesn't overpower.

〰〰〰〰〰〰〰〰〰〰〰〰〰〰 **MAKES 1 MEDIUM LOAF** 〰〰〰〰〰〰〰〰〰〰〰〰〰〰

1 cup medium grind cornmeal

1 cup teff flour

1 cup buckwheat flour

½ cup millet flour

1 tablespoon molasses

1 teaspoon sea salt, plus more for sprinkling

2 cups room temperature filtered water

1 tablespoon pumpkin seeds

1 tablespoon poppy seeds

1 tablespoon sesame seeds

1. In a large mixing bowl, thoroughly combine the cornmeal, teff flour, buckwheat flour, millet flour, molasses, salt, and water. Cover loosely with a linen cloth and let rest in a warm spot (about 70 degrees F) for at least 10 to 12 hours, or up to 24 hours.

2. Preheat the oven to 350 degrees F. Lightly grease an 8-by-4-by-4-inch loaf pan and dust with teff flour.

3. Pour the batter into the prepared pan and smooth evenly with a spatula. Top with the seeds and sea salt. Bake for 1 hour and 45 minutes, until firm to the touch and a toothpick inserted into the center comes out clean.

Cornmeal Batter Bread

This hearty cornmeal bread conjures up ideas about what it may have been like in the days of "home on the range." Quite simple and with a slight resemblance to steamed Boston bread, it has a mild flavor, but the crumb is heavy and hearty. I adore the bit of texture the cornmeal lends to this all-purpose loaf; it makes a terrific base for sandwiches or toast, and pairs well with just about any soup.

◇◇◇◇◇◇◇◇◇◇◇◇◇◇◇◇◇◇◇◇◇◇◇◇ **MAKES 1 MEDIUM LOAF** ◇◇◇◇◇◇◇◇◇◇◇◇◇◇◇◇◇◇◇◇◇◇◇◇

2 cups teff flour

1 cup medium grind cornmeal, plus additional for sprinkling

½ cup millet flour

1 tablespoon molasses

1 teaspoon sea salt, plus additional for sprinkling

2 cups room temperature filtered water

1. In a large mixing bowl, combine all of the ingredients thoroughly. Cover loosely with a linen cloth and let rest in a warm spot (about 70 degrees F) for at least 10 to 12 hours, or up to 24 hours.

2. Preheat the oven to 350 degrees F. Lightly grease an 8-by-4-by-4-inch loaf pan and dust with cornmeal.

3. Pour the batter into the prepared pan and smooth evenly with a spatula. Sprinkle with cornmeal and sea salt. Bake for 1 hour and 45 minutes, until firm to the touch and a toothpick inserted into the center comes out clean.

✦ Sesame Seed Batter Bread ✦

This batter bread is a smidgen sweeter than the other batter breads here with the small but significant addition of maple syrup. And the texture, while still heavy, is without the heartiness the cornmeal lends to my other batter breads. Thinly sliced pieces are amazing with cashew cheese and a glass of chilled white wine.

◇◇◇◇◇◇◇◇◇◇◇◇◇◇◇◇◇◇ **MAKES 1 MEDIUM LOAF** ◇◇◇◇◇◇◇◇◇◇◇◇◇◇◇◇◇◇

2 cups teff flour

½ cup sesame seeds, plus additional for sprinkling

½ cup quinoa flour

½ cup amaranth flour

½ cup millet flour

1 tablespoon molasses

1½ teaspoons maple syrup

1 teaspoon sea salt, plus additional for sprinkling

2 cups room temperature filtered water

1. In a large mixing bowl combine all of the ingredients thoroughly. Cover loosely with a linen cloth and let rest in a warm spot (about 70 degrees F) for at least 10 to 12 hours, or up to 24 hours.

2. Preheat the oven to 350 degrees F. Lightly grease an 8-by-4-by-4-inch loaf pan and dust with teff flour.

3. Pour the batter into the prepared pan and smooth evenly with a spatula. Top with additional sesame seeds and sea salt. Bake for 1 hour and 45 minutes, until firm to the touch and a toothpick inserted into the center comes out clean.

QUICK BREADS

QUICK BREADS HAVE A WONDERFULLY TENDER, muffin-like texture and quality. They require the enjoyable labor of mixing ingredients together, pouring a rich and somewhat thin batter into a loaf pan, and patiently waiting while it bakes into a gratifying loaf of goodness. In most cases, the quick bread recipes here have been created to be slightly sweet, as I imagine them being fancied for breakfast or with afternoon tea.

Quick breads are a modern pleasure because their main leavening agent, baking soda, was invented fairly recently. When naturally occurring, it is known as *nahcolite*. Mined since ancient times, nahcolite has actually been used as a cleanser. It has only been within the last 170 years that baking soda has been used as a leavener in baking. It was in 1847, when two bakers discovered that $NaHCO_3$, when combined with a liquid and a touch of something acidic (such as lemon juice), created carbon dioxide bubbles. These two bakers invented the manufactured form of baking soda that we predominantly use in our baking today.

The leavening that baking soda creates when added to my batters yields a unique kind of lightness and tenderness due to the many carbon dioxide bubbles making their way through the dough, creating countless little holes. As I mentioned above, baking soda is activated by a touch of something acidic, but it is also called to action with heat. So even if there is not much acid in a batter, the heat from the oven will activate the baking soda, which aerates the exquisite quick breads and gives them a lovely rise.

All the recipes in this section are slightly sweet, with the exception of the Quick Anadama Bread (page 146). I believe this just might be the first quick bread rendition of the classic yeasted corn bread. While looking into the beginnings of this tasty bread, I discovered a perfectly hilarious account of how the first Anadama bread came to be, as well as its title. Apparently, a local Rockport, Massachusetts, fisherman had the unfortunate circumstance of coming home to the same repetitive dinner, night after night: steamed cornmeal mush sweetened with a tad of molasses. So one evening the fellow comes home and, feeling more than a little perturbed at yet another plate of mush staring up at him for another boring supper, he decides to take matters into his own hands. So he mixes the mush with bread flour and yeast, pops it into the oven, and proclaims, "Anna damn her!" What results is an extraordinary loaf of the most delicious bread. Word spreads, and neighbors begin baking the same bread, calling it Anadama bread. While developing my gluten-free vegan version, no one was "damned," but I almost wish I had cause to, just to carry on the tradition.

For all the other quick breads, I use a variety of sweeteners such as date sugar, maple syrup, Sucanat, and evaporated cane juice. I try to keep the amount of sugar to a minimum while still creating a tasty, slightly sweet loaf. The Blueberry Streusel Bread (page 149) is an exception and calls for a fair amount of maple syrup. But oh my, it is just right for the recipe! As a sweeter treat that is still full of nutrition, it will knock your socks off! The Apple Walnut Bread (page 157) is laden with apple chunks and is so satisfying, but significantly less sweet than the blueberry bread. These quick bread recipes offer a lot of variety with flavor combinations as well as composition. If you feel like creating your own loaves with different fruit and nut combinations, the Raspberry-Rooibos Tea Bread (page 155), Peach Ginger Bread (page 145), and Blueberry Streusel Bread (page 149) recipes offer terrific bases to experiment with.

Quick Bread Tips and Techniques

These breads come together quickly! So here are a few tips to take with you into this chapter; they are all fairly standard baking tips.

First things first! It is always a good idea to start with preheating your oven and lightly greasing your baking pan. With the exception of three rounded free-form breads, all of the recipes here are baked in an 8-by-4-by-4-inch loaf pan. To be organized and to have what I call a "zen baking experience," I recommend measuring all the ingredients in advance. So, next in order comes measuring the dry ingredients. Simply combine well in one bowl and set aside. Next measure out and combine the wet ingredients in a large mixing bowl (if you are using a stand mixer, go ahead and use that mixing bowl for your wet ingredients). Then direct your attention to the measuring, chopping, and setting aside of the nuts, fresh fruits, dried fruits, frozen berries, and other add-ins. After all of your ingredients are measured and in their appointed bowls, it is time to swiftly combine them. With your mixer on low or with your mixing arm on low speed, start incorporating the dry ingredients into the wet. When they are well combined and have a thick batter consistency, fold in the additional yummy chopped nuts, fruits, and the like. Pour this completed quick bread batter into the prepared loaf pan and place in your hot oven. Wait for these quick breads to cool for about 1 hour before slicing: doing so ensures a lovely cakelike crumb, whereas if you slice the bread when it is still hot, the texture will be less favorable, being somewhat gummy and too moist. It is just fine to let it cool in its baking pan.

You will notice that the Apple Walnut Bread (page 157), Banana Walnut Bread (page 147), and Cranberry Pecan Bread (page 152) batters are thicker than the other quick bread batters, which are quite thin. The Holiday Irish Soda Bread (page 156) and Quick Anadama Bread (page 146) are more dough-like than typical quick bread batters.

There is not much else to it! Enjoy!

✦ Peach Ginger Bread ✦

I make this bread with white peaches when they are in season and serve it warm for dessert with homemade vanilla-cashew ice cream. Frozen peaches (thawed beforehand) or other fresh fruits can be used with scrumptious and satisfactory results. The ginger is subtle and not overpowering. If you are looking for more intensity, add some freshly grated, peeled, fresh gingerroot to the batter. Please do not be alarmed that this dough/batter is indeed more batter-like and quite thin. When the bread pops out of the oven and has cooled slightly, you will be delighted with its exquisite tea bread consistency and lovely taste.

◇◇◇◇◇◇◇◇◇◇◇◇◇◇◇◇◇◇◇ **MAKES 1 MEDIUM LOAF** ◇◇◇◇◇◇◇◇◇◇◇◇◇◇◇◇◇◇◇

1½ cups teff flour

½ cup tapioca flour

¼ cup arrowroot

1½ teaspoons baking soda

1 teaspoon ground cinnamon

¾ teaspoon sea salt

½ teaspoon ground ginger

¾ cup maple syrup

½ cup coconut oil

1½ teaspoons vanilla extract

1 cup room temperature
   filtered water

1 cup white peach, peeled
   and chopped

1. Preheat the oven to 375 degrees F. Lightly grease an 8-by-4-by-4-inch loaf pan and dust with brown rice flour or teff flour.

2. In a medium bowl, combine the teff flour, tapioca flour, arrowroot, baking soda, cinnamon, salt, and ginger.

3. In a separate large bowl (or the bowl of a stand mixer), combine the maple syrup, coconut oil, vanilla extract, and water. Add the dry ingredients and mix well by hand with a whisk or on low in the mixer, breaking up any lumps of flour. Once a smooth batter is achieved, fold in the peach pieces.

4. Pour the batter into the prepared loaf pan. Bake for 1 hour and 10 minutes, until golden and firm to the touch, and a toothpick inserted into the center comes out clean.

✦ Quick Anadama Bread ✦

I created this autumn loaf on a cold day when I had a strong need for the instant gratification that could only come from a hearty loaf of bread, rich with cornmeal and the mellow taste of molasses. In hindsight I realized that this recipe creates a beautiful loaf reminiscent of the New England Anadama bread. My version is leavened with baking soda rather than the yeast of the traditional bread, which also uses more white flour. That aside, I thought the breads' commonalities of molasses, cornmeal, a touch of oil, and a taste of the harvest season warranted a shared name. Served with cashew butter, the bread is now a family favorite.

◇◇◇◇◇◇◇◇◇◇◇◇◇◇◇◇◇◇◇◇◇ **MAKES 1 MEDIUM LOAF** ◇◇◇◇◇◇◇◇◇◇◇◇◇◇◇◇◇◇◇◇◇

1½ cups teff flour

1 cup sorghum flour

½ cup medium grind cornmeal, plus additional 2 tablespoons for shaping the dough

¼ cup flax meal

1 teaspoon baking soda

1 teaspoon xanthan gum

½ teaspoon sea salt

2 tablespoons extra-virgin olive oil

1 tablespoon molasses

1¼ cups room temperature filtered water

1. Preheat the oven to 350 degrees F. Lightly grease a sheet pan.

2. In a medium bowl, combine the teff flour, sorghum flour, ½ cup cornmeal, flax meal, baking soda, xanthan gum, and salt.

3. In a separate large bowl (or the bowl of a stand mixer), combine the olive oil, molasses, and water. Add the dry ingredients and mix well by hand or with the mixer until well combined.

4. With the additional cornmeal sprinkled on your work surface, shape the dough into a round. Place on the prepared sheet pan and score with a crisscross pattern. Bake for 1 hour and 20 minutes, until golden and firm to the touch.

✦ Banana Walnut Bread ✦

This recipe was created for my holiday cookbook but has been such a hit I felt it would be a good idea to include it here. What is so extraordinary about this banana bread is the inclusion of almond meal. That simple addition adds such moistness, and a lovely crumb. Plus I love baking with olive oil; it lends such a delicate yet distinctive sweetness.

◇◇◇◇◇◇◇◇◇◇◇◇◇◇◇◇◇◇◇◇◇◇◇◇◇ **MAKES 1 LARGE LOAF** ◇◇◇◇◇◇◇◇◇◇◇◇◇◇◇◇◇◇◇◇◇◇◇◇

2 cups teff flour

½ cup almond meal

1 teaspoon baking soda

¾ teaspoon sea salt

½ teaspoon cinnamon

2 ripe bananas, mashed

½ cup date sugar

½ cup extra-virgin olive oil

1½ teaspoons vanilla extract

½ cup room temperature filtered water

1 cup chopped walnuts

1. Preheat oven to 350 degrees F. Grease an 8-by-4-by-4-inch loaf pan and dust with teff flour.

2. In a large bowl, combine the teff flour, almond meal, baking soda, salt, and cinnamon.

3. In a separate large bowl (or the bowl of a stand mixer), combine the bananas, date sugar, olive oil, and vanilla to a smooth consistency. Add the dry ingredients and water and combine. Stir in the walnuts.

4. Pour the batter into the prepared loaf pan and bake for 1 hour, until golden and firm to the touch.

◆ Zucchini Bread ◆

Zucchini bread with date sugar is an exceptional treat. The dates lend a caramel-like sweetness that I find unique—more full bodied and earthy than other sugars. Though this bread is less sweet than most, it is satisfying in a warming way that still speaks the language of treats.

〜〜〜〜〜〜〜〜〜〜〜〜〜〜〜〜〜〜 **MAKES 1 MEDIUM LOAF** 〜〜〜〜〜〜〜〜〜〜〜〜〜〜〜〜〜〜

1 cup boiling water	1 teaspoon ground cinnamon
¾ cup date sugar	1 teaspoon baking soda
1 medium zucchini	1 teaspoon xanthan gum
¾ cup sorghum flour	¾ teaspoon sea salt
¾ cup teff flour	½ cup extra-virgin olive oil
½ cup tapioca flour	1½ teaspoons vanilla extract
¼ cup arrowroot	¾ cup walnuts, coarsely chopped

1. Preheat the oven to 350 degrees F. Lightly grease an 8-by-4-by-4-inch loaf pan and dust with brown rice flour or teff flour. In a small bowl, pour the boiling water over the date sugar and mix until the date sugar is mostly dissolved.

2. With your food processor or handheld grater, grate the zucchini. This will yield about ¾ cup, loosely packed.

3. In a medium bowl, combine the sorghum flour, teff flour, tapioca flour, arrowroot, cinnamon, baking soda, xanthan gum, and salt.

4. In a separate large bowl (or the bowl of a stand mixer), combine the date sugar mixed with hot water, the olive oil, and vanilla extract. Add the dry ingredients and mix well by hand with a whisk or with the mixer, breaking up any lumps of flour. Once a smooth batter is achieved, fold in the walnuts and grated zucchini.

5. Pour the batter into the prepared loaf pan. Bake for 1 hour and 15 minutes, until golden and firm to the touch, and a toothpick inserted into the center comes out clean.

✦ Blueberry Streusel Bread ✦

This sweet quick bread reminds me of coffee cake! It is moist and full of juicy blueberries, with a delicious streusel filling and topping. It is sweet and rich enough to serve as a dessert (perhaps à la mode), and I love the way it slices so easily and presents so beautifully on the plate.

◇◇◇◇◇◇◇◇◇◇◇◇◇◇◇◇◇◇◇◇◇ **MAKES 1 MEDIUM LOAF** ◇◇◇◇◇◇◇◇◇◇◇◇◇◇◇◇◇◇◇◇◇

STREUSEL
½ cup walnuts
⅓ cup gluten-free oats
¼ cup packed brown sugar
¼ cup extra-virgin olive oil
½ teaspoon ground cinnamon

BATTER
1½ cups teff flour
½ cup sorghum flour
¼ cup brown rice flour

1½ teaspoons baking soda
1 teaspoon ground cinnamon
¾ teaspoon sea salt
1 cup room temperature
   filtered water
1 cup maple syrup
½ cup canola oil
1½ teaspoons vanilla extract
1 cup blueberries, fresh

1. Preheat the oven to 375 degrees F. Lightly grease an 8-by-4-by-4-inch loaf pan and dust with brown rice flour or teff flour.

2. To make the streusel, pulse the walnuts, oats, brown sugar, olive oil, and cinnamon in a food processor to a coarse crumb.

3. To make the batter, in a medium bowl, combine the teff flour, sorghum flour, brown rice flour, baking soda, cinnamon, and salt.

4. In a separate large bowl (or the bowl of a stand mixer), combine the water, maple syrup, canola oil, and vanilla extract. Add the dry ingredients and mix well with a whisk by hand or the mixer, breaking up any lumps of flour. Once a smooth batter is achieved, fold in the blueberries.

5. Pour half of the batter into the prepared loaf pan. Sprinkle half of the streusel on top. Pour the remaining batter on top, then finish with the remaining streusel. Bake for 1 hour and 30 minutes, until the top is golden and firm and a toothpick inserted beneath the streusel layer comes out clean.

✦ Cranberry Pecan Bread ✦

Here is a bread that has wintery holiday flavor without being overly sweet. I love the way the sweet potato adds moistness and body to this satisfying loaf, which is so full of delectable bits of toasty pecans and sweet bursts of dried cranberries. The little bit of orange zest just whispers citrus, while the cinnamon sings a warming tune throughout each delicious bite.

◇◇◇◇◇◇◇◇◇◇◇◇◇◇◇◇◇◇◇◇◇◇◇◇ **MAKES 1 MEDIUM LOAF** ◇◇◇◇◇◇◇◇◇◇◇◇◇◇◇◇◇◇◇◇◇◇◇◇

1½ cups teff flour

½ cup flax meal

½ cup tapioca flour

1 teaspoon baking soda

1 teaspoon xanthan gum

¾ teaspoon sea salt

¾ teaspoon ground cinnamon

1 cup sweet potato purée

½ cup extra-virgin olive oil

½ cup room temperature filtered water

½ cup Sucanat

1 teaspoon grated orange zest

1½ teaspoons vanilla extract

1 cup lightly toasted pecans, chopped

½ cup dried cranberries

1. Preheat the oven to 350 degrees F. Lightly grease an 8-by-4-by-4-inch loaf pan and dust with teff flour.

2. In a medium bowl, combine the teff flour, flax meal, tapioca flour, baking soda, xanthan gum, salt, and cinnamon.

3. In a separate large bowl (or the bowl of a stand mixer), combine the sweet potato purée, olive oil, water, Sucanat, orange zest, and vanilla extract. Add the dry ingredients and mix well by hand with a whisk or with the mixer, breaking up any lumps of flour. Once a smooth batter is achieved, fold in the pecans and cranberries.

4. Pour the batter into the prepared loaf pan. Bake for 1 hour and 30 minutes, until golden and slightly firm to the touch and a toothpick inserted into the center comes out clean.

✦ Date Oat Bread ✦

My daughter loves to call this "cake bread." Let it be known this is most certainly not a cake. It's not fluffy and light; it is substantial and fibrous, robust with oats. But the sweet, caramel-like morsels of gooey dates throughout give the gift of manna to the taste buds, which reminds Lilli of cake. I go crazy over a warm slice of this bread spread thickly with tahini.

◇◇◇◇◇◇◇◇◇◇◇◇◇◇◇◇◇◇◇◇◇◇ **MAKES 1 MEDIUM ROUND** ◇◇◇◇◇◇◇◇◇◇◇◇◇◇◇◇◇◇◇◇◇◇

2½ cups teff flour

1 cup gluten-free oats, plus ½ cup additional for shaping the bread

¾ cup chopped dates

1 teaspoon xanthan gum

1 teaspoon baking soda

½ teaspoon sea salt

2 tablespoons extra-virgin olive oil

2 teaspoons evaporated cane juice

1½ cups room temperature filtered water

1. Preheat the oven to 350 degrees F. Lightly grease a sheet pan.

2. In a medium bowl, combine the teff flour, 1 cup oats, dates, xanthan gum, baking soda, and salt.

3. In a separate large bowl (or the bowl of a stand mixer), combine the olive oil, cane juice, and water. Add the dry ingredients and mix well with the mixer on low speed, or by hand until well combined.

4. Shape into a round using the additional oats sprinkled on your work surface. Place the shaped bread on the prepared sheet pan and score with a crisscross pattern. Bake for 1 hour and 10 minutes, until golden and firm to the touch.

✦ Raspberry–Rooibos Tea Bread ✦

The taste of raspberries baked into a slightly sweet quick bread conjures up memories of devouring warm raspberry muffins while on break from my very first bakery job. I was the dishwasher, twelve years old and elbow-deep in hot, steamy, soapy water, washing the many muffin tins and surrounded by the comforting smell of fresh baked goods. When it came time for me to choose my one cherished treat of the morning, without fail the raspberry muffin won out. This bread is light and sweet and much like tea bread. The delicious and healthful rooibos (red bush) herb, which has a unique sweetness all on its own, imbues a slightly nutty flavor to the bread.

◇◇◇◇◇◇◇◇◇◇◇◇◇◇◇◇◇◇◇◇◇ **MAKES 1 MEDIUM LOAF** ◇◇◇◇◇◇◇◇◇◇◇◇◇◇◇◇◇◇◇◇◇

1½ cups teff flour

¾ cup tapioca flour

1½ teaspoons baking soda

¾ teaspoon sea salt

1 cup brewed rooibos tea

½ cup coconut oil

½ cup evaporated cane juice

1½ teaspoons vanilla extract

1½ cups fresh raspberries

1. Preheat the oven to 375 degrees F. Lightly grease an 8-by-4-by-4-inch loaf pan and dust with teff flour.

2. In a medium bowl, combine the teff flour, tapioca flour, baking soda, and salt.

3. In a separate large bowl (or the bowl of a stand mixer), combine the tea, coconut oil, cane juice, and vanilla extract. Add the dry ingredients and mix well by hand with a whisk or with the mixer, breaking up any lumps of flour. Once a smooth batter is achieved, fold in the raspberries.

4. Pour the batter into the prepared loaf pan. Bake for 1 hour and 10 minutes, until golden and slightly firm to the touch, and a toothpick inserted into the center comes out clean.

✦ Holiday Irish Soda Bread ✦

Here is another recipe you will find in my holiday cookbook—but again I feel it is such a treasured recipe that it ought to be included here for those who are not familiar with it. Growing up, this was a bread I looked forward to every Saint Patrick's Day. Irish soda bread was a staple in my grandmother Noreen's house in Cleveland, Ohio, and after moving to the West Coast, my mother would continue the tradition every spring. This is my gluten-free and vegan version.

◇◇◇◇◇◇◇◇◇◇◇◇◇◇◇◇◇◇◇◇◇◇ **MAKES 1 MEDIUM LOAF** ◇◇◇◇◇◇◇◇◇◇◇◇◇◇◇◇◇◇◇◇◇◇

3 cups teff flour

2 teaspoons date sugar

1 teaspoon xanthan gum

1 teaspoon baking soda

½ teaspoon caraway seeds

½ teaspoon sea salt

½ cup dark raisins

2 tablespoons canola oil

1 cup room temperature
filtered water

1. Preheat the oven to 350 degrees F. Lightly grease a sheet pan and dust with teff flour.

2. Combine the teff flour, date sugar, xanthan gum, baking soda, caraway seeds, and salt in a large mixing bowl. Stir in the raisins. Add the oil and water and mix well until a smooth dough is formed. Gently knead the dough with just a few turns on a work surface dusted with rice flour.

3. Shape into a round loaf and score with a crisscross pattern. Put on the prepared sheet pan and bake for 50 minutes, until golden and firm to the touch.

✦ Apple Walnut Bread ✦

A gallant apple bread heartily beckons one to sit and enjoy a warm slice, any time of day. The soft apple pieces, crunchy bits of walnuts, and sweet cinnamon are surrounded by a soft and wholesome bread dough. I very much appreciate this recipe because I revel in being able to serve sweets to my family which are so enjoyable, yet not excessively full of sugary ingredients.

〰〰〰〰〰〰〰〰〰〰〰〰 **MAKES 1 LARGE LOAF** 〰〰〰〰〰〰〰〰〰〰〰〰

1 cup teff flour

½ cup flax meal

½ cup garbanzo bean flour

½ cup brown rice flour

1½ teaspoons ground cinnamon

1 teaspoon baking soda

¾ teaspoon sea salt

½ cup extra-virgin olive oil

½ cup mashed ripe banana

½ cup date sugar

2 teaspoons vanilla extract

1½ cups room temperature filtered water

1 cup chopped walnuts

1 large apple, such as Honeycrisp or Fuji, finely chopped

1. Preheat the oven to 350 degrees F. Lightly grease an 8-by-4-by-4-inch loaf pan and dust with brown rice flour or teff flour.

2. In a large bowl, combine the teff flour, flax meal, garbanzo bean flour, brown rice flour, cinnamon, baking soda, and salt.

3. In a separate large bowl (or the bowl of a stand mixer), combine the olive oil, banana, date sugar, and vanilla; mix to a smooth consistency. Mix in the dry ingredients and the water. Gently fold in the walnuts and apples.

4. Pour the batter into the prepared loaf pan and bake for 1 hour 30 minutes, until golden and firm to the touch, and a toothpick inserted into the center comes out clean.

INDEX

About the
AUTHOR

Photo by Rachelle Longé

JENNIFER KATZINGER and her father first opened the doors of the Flying Apron Bakery in 2002, recognizing the value in organic, gluten-free, vegan, and sustainable whole foods years in advance of what has become a rapidly growing industry. After growing the bakery from a tiny take-out window in Seattle's University District to a spacious and lovely café in the city's Fremont neighborhood, Jennifer sold the bakery in 2010, and it continues to thrive.

After selling the bakery, Jennifer pursued her two greatest passions: being a mother, and continuing to develop delicious and healthy recipes. She is delighted to bring you her third cookbook! Knowing delicious, wholesome bread is often the most missed food for those avoiding gluten, she is thrilled to share these new recipes. Her daughter, one of her greatest joys, was by her side in the kitchen every day, helping or napping, as Jennifer created the healthful artisan bread recipes that fill this cookbook.

Jennifer earned a BA in English Literature from the University of Washington, and pursued a Master's in Industrial Design from the Pratt Institute in Brooklyn, New York. She lives in Seattle with her husband, Joseph; their daughter, Lillian; and their dog, Neve. They enjoy taking long walks through the beautiful parks of the Pacific Northwest and creating delicious, nurturing food together.